Effective
School Board
Meetings

EFFECTIVE

SCHOOL BOARD

MEETINGS

Jack L. Davidson

Parker Publishing Company, Inc.

West Nyack, New York

LIBRARY OF CONGRESS
CATALOG CARD NUMBER: 70-106456

PRINTED IN THE UNITED STATES OF AMERICA
B & P—0-13-245316-9

About This Book

This book is prepared as an aid to superintendents and board members as they work to effect sound decisions for education through carefully planned, productive meetings. Since official actions of the Board occur only at regularly constituted meetings, it is important that procedures be established to ensure an efficient operation.

School Boards, like the individuals comprising them, vary considerably from one school system to another. No two are alike. Some contain agreeable, amiable people who relate well to other members of the Board and to the community; some contain individuals whose primary function seems to be one of producing the maximum amount of discord and discontent. Some Boards conduct only routine business, some work constantly in a state of emergency and duress. Some Boards meet in relative tranquility without a large audience, while others meet surrounded by the press, radio, television, and constant pressure groups of varying sizes and complexities. To attempt the establishment of a set of rules or procedures for the conducting of board meetings in all these circumstances is to attempt the impossible. Yet it is obvious that certain factors tend to produce more effective meetings while certain other factors tend to help create confusion and disorder. The intent of this book is to describe items which may be helpful in some circumstances, in some areas, under some conditions, to provide more productive school board meetings.

The success of most school board meetings is dependent upon the amount and quality of the planning that precedes the meeting. The superintendent of schools bears a major responsibility for this planning along with the chairman of the Board of Education and members of the superintendent's staff. How the superintendent utilizes the talents of his team of staff members has a direct bearing on the outcome of the meeting. No superintendent today can function effectively in isolation. The times we live in make this impractical. Neither can the superintendent abdicate his decision making powers, for administration by committee is administration by confusion and indecision.

It is generally true that the major decisions concerning local school systems are made during meetings of the Board of Education. The circumstances surrounding those meetings, and the preparations that preceded them, have profound effects on the types of decisions that are made.

A Board of Education develops a personality in much the same way that an individual develops a personality. The image the Board builds within the community and the area develops from the actions taken by the Board. Fairness, thoroughness, free expression of beliefs and convictions, an honest recognition of differences of opinion, and a common belief in providing quality education are necessary ingredients to a successful school board operation. No lay citizen participates in a more important activity. The effectiveness with which that task is fulfilled has great implications for the future.

J. L. Davidson

Table of Contents

7

Effective
School Board
Meetings

1

Establishing the Foundation for Effective Planning

Serving on a Board of Education represents one of the finest contributions an individual can make to his community. As education assumes an increasingly important role in our society, the effectiveness with which Boards of Education operate becomes increasingly important. Citizens look to the Board of Education for thoughful consideration and decisive action on problems which affect the entire community. Every meeting of the Board of Education helps to establish the image and the reputation of that Board. Some Boards develop a reputation for forthright decisions, others seem to find great difficulty in moving the educational system with authority and precision.

Official actions of the Board of Education can be taken only in regularly constituted meetings of the Board. Individual members have no authority outside of these meetings. It stands to reason that these meetings must be carefully planned and properly conducted in order to expedite the tremendously important business of education in the local community. Poorly planned meetings often result in indecision and confusion, and cause the public to view the Board, and the entire school system, with doubt and suspicion instead of confidence and respect.

In most cases planning for effective school board meetings is the responsibility primarily of the superintendent of schools and his staff. There is a direct relationship between the caliber of this planning and the effectiveness of the meeting. This chapter is concerned primarily with this staff planning and outlines some suggestions to make this planning more effective.

TEAM APPROACH

The concept of the "superintendency" is accepted by an increasing number of school superintendents today. This concept pictures the superintendent of schools as the captain of a team of staff members working together in dealing with the problems of the school system. The superintendent is no longer pictured as an individual sitting in an office by himself and making decisions which direct the school system in a unilateral way. As with all management today, the superintendent of schools is developing into a position of leadership that requires teamwork and co-ordinated efforts. Education is so complex today, even in the smallest of school systems, that it is impossible for a superintendent to operate in isolation. He cannot carry the total responsibility for all decisions without consultation, advice, and assistance from members of his staff. This is not intended to mean that the super-intendent abdicates his decision making authority or that all administration must be accomplished through group participation because school systems cannot be operated successfully by com-mittees alone. Someone must make the ultimate decision and that responsibility rests squarely on the shoulders of the superintendent. In the process of arriving at a decision the superintendent must call on the available personnel and resources in order to make an intel-ligent decision to deal with the problem at hand. Planning for meetings of the Board of Education can be accomplished most effectively with this team approach.

One of the first tasks of the superintendent is to establish the team approach with his entire administration. This holds true not only for planning effective school board meetings but for dealing with all of the major problems facing his school system. The super-intendent must bear the direct responsibility for creating an ad-ministrative atmosphere in which staff members can function as members of the team. Members of the staff must feel secure in this relationship and must understand their roles and responsibilities in making the relationship effective.

Selecting the Team

As the superintendent contemplates the planning processes for meetings of the Board of Education, he must first select his plan-ning team. The size of this team will vary from one school system to another depending upon the size of the system and its complexity.

In general, the team should be small enough to be effective yet large enough to be comprehensive and inclusive. In most instances the team should consist of those staff members having ultimate responsibility in various areas of operation. Generally this would include assistant superintendents in charge of specific functions such as: instruction, business, personnel, administration, and other areas. Since all school systems vary in their organization and structure, the superintendent can best decide the makeup of this team. In some instances this team might consist of only two or three top management personnel, while in others, the team might consist of as many as a dozen members. The size of this group is not dependent totally on the size of the school system but rather upon the organizational structure and on the personnel themselves. Some staff members who work close to the superintendent may not be included on this team while others who work in a different relationship may be very valuable members of the team. The composition of the planning team will depend a great deal on how the superintendent plans to use his staff during the board meeting. Some superintendents prefer to handle all facets of the school program themselves during the actual meetings. Others prefer to turn over various aspects of the school operation to the director or supervisor of that area for reporting to the Board of Education. The actual involvement of the staff member in a board meeting must be determined and understood by all concerned. If the superintendent does not wish for staff members to be actual participants in the meeting, this should be made clear to the staff members. In this case they would generally respond to the questions only at the invitation of the superintendent. The board members should understand the procedure the superintendent would like to follow in this matter with members of his staff and should respect his wishes. There is no pat answer to the structure of this planning team but it will be apparent to most superintendents that those with ultimate responsibility should definitely be members of this group.

A point should be made here concerning the security for members of the planning team. It is important that the members of the planning team feel that they not only have specific responsibilities in preparing for meetings of the Board of Education, but that once given a task, the completion of this task will not be interfered with by the superintendent. Certainly the superintendent will hold the staff member responsible for the successful completion of the task, but he will not be constantly directing him in how it should be done. The superintendent will make clear in the beginning how the report should be prepared and feel free to request additions or deletions, but should use good judgment in working on the security of the staff member in his position. The delegation of responsibility also implies the delegation of authority to complete the task.

Establishing Procedures

After the members of the team have been determined, the next step is to establish procedures to be followed in planning for effective meetings of the Board of Education. These procedures should be consistent with the overall philosophy of administration in the school system. The superintendent should call together the members of his team and discuss with them the procedures that should be adopted. In determining these procedures it is well to have in mind the desired outcome or goals of the school board meetings. It is at this stage of the preliminary planning that discussions should occur concerning the internal operations of the school system. It is necessary to discuss at least the following problems:

1. Meeting dates
2. Time for mailing of agendas to members of the Board
3. Deadlines for preparation
4. Style for completion of materials

In discussing the dates of regular meetings, a board calendar should be prepared which outlines the dates of the regular meetings of the Board for the entire year. This calendar should include every regularly established meeting, those special meetings known to be required, and other important dates on which the Board of Education will convene. The board calendar can be of real assistance to members of the Board as they plan their activities for the year. Special meetings such as budget review sessions, tentative dates for negotiations, commencement exercises, and other school-wide activities are important for the board members. This board calendar is important in laying the foundation for long range planning, which will be discussed later.

Timing is an extremely important part of the planning stage for school board meetings. The planning team should determine the dates and times when certain aspects of the preparation should be completed. Most superintendents and board members agree that materials for the agenda should be delivered to board members prior to the meeting in order to allow sufficient time for study of the materials of business. The planning team should determine, in cooperation with the board members, the number of days prior to the meeting that the agenda materials will be delivered. In arriving at this schedule the planning team must then determine the final day when materials must be ready. Specific problem areas should be discussed. For example: If bids for certain goods or services are to be reviewed by the Board of Education, the staff must be aware of the meeting date in order to allow sufficient time for bid proposals to be mailed, bids to be received, study made of these bids, and recommendations made on the bids.

Using a specific example, we will assume that the Board of Education meets regularly on the first Thursday of each month at 9 A.M. Looking at the question of pre-planning, agendas and all supporting materials should be mailed or delivered to the Board on the previous Friday. Allowing three days for typing, mimeographing, and compiling all materials, this would establish Tuesday as the deadline for all materials that will appear on the agenda. This means in effect that such matters as competitive bids, advertising and receipt of bids must be accomplished approximately ten days prior to the meeting for board action. If this will produce special problems in the school system, the planning team should take notice of these special circumstances and provide procedures for meeting these circumstances.

Every school system will have special circumstances that require attention of the planning team. These might include the utilization of special talents of staff members involved in the planning of the agenda, and the recognition of certain deficiencies that might occur. Care should be given so that office staff members are not given responsibilities for which they are not prepared. It is not always efficient to assign responsibilities in certain areas simply because they fall within the internal confines of that specified responsibility. Other special circumstances must be identified by the superintendent and the planning team and taken into consideration during the planning process.

Fixing Responsibilities

Commensurate with the establishment of procedures for planning should be the determination of responsibilities. Each member of the planning team should bear a specific responsibility for the planning and preparation of materials and information involved in the meetings of the Board of Education. At this point it should be emphasized again that school systems will vary considerably in how these responsibilities can be assigned. However this is done by the planning team, the assignment of responsibilities should be clear to all involved. There should be no doubt as to the responsibility for such matters as report on curriculum, personnel, business, student welfare, and the like. It must be spelled out also who bears the responsibility for final approval of various portions of the agenda and for the actual preparation of backup materials. It should be clear that the superintendent gives final approval to the total agenda prior to compilation and mailing.

If materials for the meeting are prepared by different departments or divisions within the school system, care should be taken that the same procedure is followed by all departments. The same style and format should be used by all those preparing materials for the agenda. The procedures that might be followed in this regard are discussed in more detail in Chapter 3, which deals specifically with planning and developing the agenda.

Planning Sessions

The planning team should determine a tentative schedule for their planning sessions. The frequency of these sessions will depend to some extent on how often the board of education meets in regular session. The planning team should meet at least twice prior to every regular meeting of the Board. The first meeting should be a general planning session approximately two weeks prior to the time when agendas and materials will be mailed. This meeting would involve general matters of business to be conducted at the next meeting, but would also be a time for discussion of matters for future agendas. It is in these meetings that long range planning should be conducted. The staff member bearing ultimate responsibility in the area of instruction should plan ahead so that he can have a logical sequence to his reports on curriculum and instruction. This should be planned in such a way as to afford the best opportunity for continuity. In business affairs the staff member directing this area should determine the long range approach to communication with the Board. In planning for new school buildings, for example, a logical sequence of reports should be established so that the reports build on each other and provide a solid basis upon which the Board can make intelligent decisions. The planning team should develop a flexible calendar for long range planning. This calendar should be revised periodically in the light of new developments. If a long range plan for presentation to the Board of Education is not accomplished, the board finds itself simply reacting to immediate problems instead of pursuing a logically planned and systematic pattern of operation. It is the responsibility of this planning team to guide the operations of the Board by suggesting those areas which need attention over a given period of time. This should be discussed with the Board so that both the Board and the staff are aware of the long range plans which the planning team will pursue.

The second meeting of the planning team should be held just prior to the actual compilation of all materials. In this meeting specific details should be discussed and responsibilities for presentations should be cleared. There will be many occasions in which the planning team will find it helpful to meet, if only briefly, about two days before the actual meeting. At this session the team can discuss specific details of presentation, timing, expected reactions, and similar matters. It would also be worthwhile at this point to have at least some discussion on dealing with the unexpected. Almost every meeting produces some event that is unexpected in spite of the detailed planning. These unexpected events take many forms. Sometimes an irate citizen appears and demands to be heard on a specific issue without any previous conversation with the superintendent or the staff members. Even in those school systems that have definite policies concerning how a person may be heard at a meeting of the Board of Education, they can be a serious matter if the citizen is not given any consideration. This is particularly true when the citizen considers his problem to require immediate attention. Occasionally a board member will introduce a new problem at a meeting. Some board members may attempt to use the public meetings to campaign for re-election and in this vein may take off in almost any direction that is totally unexpected. Some superintendents simply assign an "X" factor to the forthcoming meeting to allow for such unexpected events. The best laid plans often go awry when the unexpected occurs. An unexpected petition delivered by a crowd of angry citizens can be disconcerting to some board members. A general rule of thumb followed by many Boards is to avoid making a decision at that moment. This general rule of thumb should be very helpful to a Board in avoiding snap decisions and judgments which might prove in the future to be costly or embarrassing. The superintendent can be of assistance in situations of this kind if he will recommend that the matter raised by the group be considered by the administration so that a recommendation will be forthcoming to the Board for action at a subsequent meeting. The Board should set a time for action on the particular situation so that it will not appear to be simply postponing the matter in order to avoid making a decision. Snap judgments in reaction to protest movements, or petitions, or assemblies of large groups, can prove quite harmful to the image of the Board. The point should be emphasized that it is important that the Board not make a hasty decision, but it is likewise important that they not postpone the decision indefinitely. Whatever form the unexpected events take, the superintendent and the planning team must take these into consideration in their future planning.

The superintendent generally establishes within the school system an operational procedure that provides for direct communication from the school system to the Board only through the superintendent. Consistent with this philosophy, most superintendents prefer to conduct the staff portions of the meeting themselves and to call on staff members for participation when it is most appropriate and helpful. This procedure is discussed in detail in Chapter 5.

Review of Procedures

It is good business for the planning team to periodically review its procedures. It should not be assumed that one set of procedures will suffice for the entire year without revision. It is good practice in a general planning session for the team to check deficiencies in the operation. Assistant superintendents, or directors, who have the ultimate responsibility for certain areas of operation, should feel an obligation to search for better ways to conduct their own responsibilities. The superintendent must provide the atmosphere in which this can happen. The superintendent can establish such an atmosphere by listening carefully to the suggestions that are made by members of the planning team and by using these suggestions whenever they are deemed appropriate. He should constantly be alert for opportunities to instill in those staff members the need for their constructive advice and contributions. When this atmosphere does exist, and team members are searching for better ways to operate, the planning procedure should consistently improve.

Review of Suggested Procedures

1. Use the team approach. The superintendent cannot operate in a vacuum.
2. The superintendent is the captain of this team and coordinates all staff planning.
3. Determine the members of the planning team.
4. Establish procedures and fix responsibilities for all team members.
5. Schedule planning sessions with an eye toward both long range and immediate planning.
6. Leave room for the unexpected.
7. Review your planning procedures periodically.

2

Producing Effective
Communication Between
the Superintendent
and the Board

Every practicing administrator realizes the tremendous importance of providing effective communication between the superintendent of schools and the Board of Education. The Board and the superintendent must work together effectively as a team in order to provide the best possible framework for a sound educational program within the school system. This framework requires that an effective method of communication be established. A major complaint of Boards of Education is that superintendents have not established a satisfactory means of communication with the individual members of the Board. Board members complain of not being informed adequately and particularly complain about lack of information regarding crucial issues which arise from time to time within the school system. It should appear clear that the superintendent must take the initiative for establishing this effective means of communication. It is one of his prime responsibilities. When one realizes that the policy making body of the school system cannot operate without adequate information, and when one accepts the philosophy that the Board communicates with the school system through the superintendent of schools, then it becomes clear that the superintendent must accept the responsibility for this communication network with the Board of Education and must establish procedures and vehicles by which this communication can be effected. This chapter is restricted primarily to communication between the superintendent and the Board as it affects meetings of the Board of Education. It is necessary, however, to reflect also on communications which are related to the meetings but not definitely involving the meetings. While it is understood by most practicing administrators that no single technique or formula will be sufficient for every school system, there are certain items to be considered as the superintendent plans for effective communications with the Board of Education, as this communication affects the meetings of that Board.

Providing the Framework

The establishment of a system of communications between the superintendent and the Board should not be established in a helter-skelter method, but should be established with a view toward long range development and understanding on the part of both the Board and the superintendent. This understanding can best be achieved by a meeting between the Board and superintendent to discuss the most effective means for informing the Board on both the operational aspects of the school system and upon the problems that are arising within the school system. In this initial meeting the superintendent can discuss with the Board the areas of concern about which the Board would like to be informed on a regular continuing basis. At this meeting the superintendent, along with the Board, should strive to develop procedures, understandings, and an atmosphere for effective communication. The procedures will vary tremendously from school to school. In some systems various methods of communication may be quite effective which would in another system not be nearly as effective. This variation occurs because of differences in the size, administrative structure, and complexities of various school systems in different parts of the country.

On the question of understandings that should exist between members of the Board and the superintendent, this appears to be a constant matter which would remain the same from one school system to another. There appears to be no question that the superintendent and the board members must come to understandings as to how the superintendent will communicate with the Board and what procedures the board members will use in communicating with the superintendent. These understandings must be jointly arrived at and must be understood by all concerned.

One of the most important elements by which to effect good communications is the development of an atmosphere of mutual trust and respect, which implies that within such atmosphere good communications can be accomplished. The superintendent and the members of the Board of Education share an equal responsibility for the establishment of this feeling of trust and understanding. No superintendent can operate effectively in the area of communications if he is in doubt about the trust, respect, and understanding of members of his Board of Education. In the same vein, no member of a Board of Education can place full confidence in the communications of the superintendent unless he respects and understands the superintendent himself both as an individual personality and as a professional administrator. It cannot be stressed too greatly that the essence of good communications requires the establishment of an atmosphere in which both parties feel a mutual trust of each other. Once this atmosphere is established, both the superintendent and the individual board members can feel free to relate to each other in such a way that when misunderstandings do occur they can be eliminated or corrected.

At this initial meeting in which the Board and the superintendent work out the framework for the establishment of good communications, it is well to discuss the procedures by which the superintendent will communicate on special occasions with the chairman of the Board. On many occasions the superintendent is obligated to provide special kinds of communication with the chairman of the Board. More will be said about this special communication between the superintendent and the chairman in a later portion of this chapter. This special meeting of the Board and the superintendent to provide the framework for effective communications should serve as a sounding board for both the members and the superintendent. The wishes of the Board should be made known and be made clear to the superintendent. They should inform the superintendent of the kinds of information they desire about the school system as those bits of information relate to future meetings of the Board. The superintendent, by the same fashion, should be able to provide the Board with the procedures by which he will communicate with the Board. The superintendent must bear in mind that in the majority of cases members of the Board of Education are lay citizens who may have little training in facing the public and in making decisions in an atmosphere which is often filled with anxiety and tension. The more information the superintendent can provide the members of the Board of

Education, and the better he can keep them continually informed, the better the chance for an effective board member. The superintendent must accept the responsibility for providing the framework and outlining that framework to the members of the Board.

Method of Communicating

Every superintendent accepts the fact that communications with the Board may be accomplished by personal contact, by the telephone, and by written messages. Each of these means of direct communication may be important at one time or another in the superintendent's program for board communication. Face-to-face contact with members of the board provides both opportunities and dangers. Almost any kind of communication can be accomplished more effectively in a personal situation than in any other fashion. Superintendents, however, face a rather peculiar problem when they communicate with individual board members in a personalized situation. It is generally accepted that the Board of Education operates only as an entity, and that individual board members have no legal standing or responsibility as individuals. They become legally and educationally effective only when they are assembled in a regularly constituted meeting of the Board. As a result of this, many superintendents refrain from direct personal contact with members of the Board. This procedure can be seriously limiting to a program of effective communication. It should be clear that in the process of providing a framework for effective communications, the superintendent should make arrangements with individual members of the Board for periodic consultation and discussion. This must be made clear to all members of the Board at one time. If this is not done there are many occasions on which board members will have the opportunity to become suspicious of communications that might be occurring in a face-to-face relationship between the superintendent and individual members of the Board. So it appears there are both opportunities and handicaps to personal communications. Most of the dangers of this kind of communication can be offset if the superintendent and the board members understand each other and operate within an atmosphere of trust and understanding that is so necessary for good communication.

The superintendent often uses the telephone as an effective means of communicating with individual board members. In emergency situations the superintendent can generally make the most direct communication with board members by phone. When an accident occurs at a school, or other emergency arises within the school system, the superintendent will generally make this known to members of the Board through the use of the telephone. The superintendent should remember that the telephone is available for direct contact with the board members, particularly on those matters which require immediate contact. Some superintendents delegate to their secretaries the chore of relating messages directly to board members over the telephone. This practice should be discouraged however, in the view of many board members. They are generally desirous of being informed directly from the superintendent when this is possible. In emergency situations, of course, and in situations of great complexity, it often is advantageous for both the superintendent and the Board to have either a secretary or an assistant contact the board members by phone for certain specific circumstances.

Written communication between the superintendent and the Board may take several forms. Regular written communication seems to be a necessity in order for the superintendent to keep the Board informed about the activities of the school system. There exists great variety in the methods of superintendents in informing the Board concerning school events, particularly as those events may relate to meetings of the Board in the near future. Some superintendents send periodical memos to board members as the situation seems to dictate. If particular problems are arising in the school system, the superintendent may communicate with the Board concerning one particular problem. He may, on the other hand, send written messages to the Board only on very special occasions. Other superintendents take quite a different viewpoint and send written memos to the Board on every matter that may require their future consideration. Still others send written messages to the Board on every major item handled by the superintendent. This is a determination which must be made by the superintendent in consort with his Board of Education so that a mutual understanding exists about the kinds of communications — written communications — which the Board can expect from the superintendent. One good procedure is for the superintendent to make a regular practice of sending a weekly memorandum to the members of the Board outlining in general form the major events of the week so that board members will have at least a general understanding of those areas which might require future attention. This also provides the board members with an up-to-date running account of the activities of the school system. In smaller systems board members like to have an understanding of particular events which might be related to them by members of the community during the week: The curriculum innovation that is changing the schedule at the high school, the bus problem that occurred last week involving three elementary schools, the fracas at the high school between groups of students, the problems of racial intergration, and many other matters which will from time to time occur in the smaller school systems. Members of the Boards of Education in larger school systems are generally concerned about other activities which occur within the school system. The superintendent, over a period of time, must become attuned to the kinds of events and information which board members desire and make every effort to either provide that information or explain to the Board why it cannot be provided. A weekly bulletin or summary to the Board of Education has real merit in that it does provide a regular consistent communication from the superintendent to the Board and provides an avenue for explaining various problems and situations that are occurring. Located at the end of this chapter is Exhibit A, an example of a regular weekly bulletin to the Board of Education. Exhibit B is an example of a special memorandum concerning an unusual event that did not fall within the realm of the weekly bulletin to the Board. In addition to the regular periodic written communications, the superintendent will certainly want to communicate with the Board on special events that occur. This is particularly true in cases in which the Board will soon be called upon to discuss the event and possibly make a decision concerning the event or circumstance.

The superintendent should be particularly concerned about the style of his written communications with the Board of Education. The communications should:

1. *Be concise.* There is no need for the superintendent to go into great detail in most written communications with the Board unless they are of a specific nature which require detailed information. Most superintendents tend to write too much and not write often enough.

2. *Refrain from using educational "jargon."* Pedagogical statements should be reserved for other kinds of communication. This is not the time to impress the Board with your educational vocabulary.

3. *Be straightforward and to the point.*

4. *Be according to a format which is consistent from one communication to the other.* This consistency may take the form of a memorandum, a bulletin from the superintendent, or some other form, but whatever the form, it should be consistent from one communication to the next. Many superintendents, in their weekly or bi-weekly bulletins to the Board, develop a format in which the general areas of operation are discussed and the important events emphasized. In this communication the superintendent might have information concerning the areas of finance, curriculum, general administration, schoolhouse construction, and special current problems which are under consideration by the administration and those which may soon become problems of the Board of Education.

Many superintendents are concerned about the advantages and disadvantages of social contacts with individual members of the Board of Education. This is an area where the superintendent needs to be especially perceptive. He cannot afford to misread the situation in relation to social contacts with individual board members. While the superintendent might accomplish a great deal in establishing better understanding with an individual board member through social activities, he may at the same time endanger his standing and reputation with other members of the Board. Some superintendents arrange social contacts with the total Board of Education at one time. This is, of course, outlawed in some states due to the open meeting clauses or Sunshine Laws. Social contacts with the total Board of Education or with individual board members can be quite rewarding in some circumstances. The superintendent and the board members must judge together the effectiveness of this kind of communication. In general, however, there are more dangers to social contacts of a deliberate nature between the superintendent and individual board members than there are advantages. It is a situation which should be approached with great care and with understanding. If ever board members, or members of the community, misread the social contacts that occur between board members and the superintendent, the result may well be a lack of harmony and understanding and may lead to a depreciation of the atmosphere which is desired by Boards and superintendents for effective communication.

Special Communication with the Chairman of the Board

The very nature of the position of chairman of the Board of Education requires special communication with the superintendent. The chairman is charged, in most situations, with the responsibility for the operation of the meeting. He must have a close working relationship with the superintendent and must have a good understanding of the problems that are to be handled on the forthcoming agenda. He must understand both the reasons for the placement of items on the agenda and the reasons for the sequence of events on the agenda. The chairman has a heavy responsibility for the conduct of the meeting. The procedures to be followed by the chairman in the operation of the meeting should be discussed in detail with the superintendent of schools. This is the time for the superintendent to inform the chairman of problem areas which he knows will arise. The board chairman and superintendent should discuss the operational techniques of the meeting that are desired by both the chairman and the superintendent, and they should have an understanding for the simple operation of the meeting. This understanding should include such things as: knowing when the chairman will discuss certain matters that relate to the agenda; at what point the superintendent will be recognized; and what kinds of reports and information the superintendent will be giving to the Board. The superintendent should explain to the chairman how he intends to use various staff members or outside experts and consultants during the board meeting so that the chairman will understand his intended procedures. During this discussion between the superintendent and the chairman, there should be time for developing and understanding of the possibilities of various emergency procedures. If the superintendent expects a pressure group to arrive at the board meeting on some special situation, the chairman of the Board should be made cognizant of this fact and they should discuss means of dealing with this group. The superintendent and the chairman should also discuss the proposed time schedule for the meeting and arrive at a conclusion as to their decisions in the event a particular subject would require more or less time than was planned on the agenda. The chairman should understand completely what action is necessary by the Board for every item on the agenda. If this is simply a matter of information for the Board, this should be made clear in the agenda materials but it should also be re-emphasized to the chairman by the superintendent. On those matters which require special action, the board chairman should know in advance the kinds of action that are required and the necessary vote needed to pass or reject those particular matters.

It is extremely important that the superintendent develop a rapport with members of the Board of Education, and with the chairman in particular, that will enable the superintendent to work more effectively in his job as executive officer of the Board. Rapport is in many ways an intangible item. It is impossible to establish a specific set of guidelines for the establishment of good rapport with members of the Board of Education, but the superintendent with good perception can soon determine whether or not the desirable rapport does exist. Through his contacts with members of the Board, and through his professional actions as superintendent, he can develop an understanding on the part of the board members as to the role he plays in the school system, the difficulties involved in the position, and the responsibilities he assumes as superintendent. He should take every precaution to treat all board members alike with professional courtesy and personal concern. He should bear in mind what to him is the most desirable relationship between the superintendent and the Board, and strive consistently to effect that kind of relationship. No one can describe specifically what that relationship ought to be for a superintendent, but a desirable rapport is necessary for the successful operation of the school system and for a relationship which is personally satisfying to the board members and to the superintendent.

The board chairman must have a particular understanding of special events that must be handled during the meeting of the Board. If bond issues are to be passed, for example, the appropriate resolution would have been prepared in advance of the meeting, but the chairman must have a special understanding of the legal requirements for the passing of the resolution and for the next legal steps to be taken. The chairman must know if the attorney is to be in attendance at the meeting and whether or not an opinion from the attorney on that particular question is desired. It should be made clear at this point that the special communications between the superintendent and the board chairman are not to be construed as a means of arriving at any pre-meeting decisions. The superintendent should exercise great care in these discussions with the chairman not to attempt to influence his decisions or his subsequent action in the meeting as they relate to specific proposals or matters of concern on the agenda. It would be a foolish superintendent indeed, who would attempt to use this method for influencing the vote of a board chairman. Board chairmen, by the same token, must be certain not to use this special period of communication as a means of influencing the superintendent as an individual board member. The ethics and professional ideals of both the superintendent and the board member require that this communication be of a type that relates entirely to the operational procedures that will be employed during the board meeting. It must be clearly understood by all other board members of education that this special communication between the superintendent and the board chairman is going to occur and what the purpose of these special meetings is. If either the board chairman or the superintendent perceive any difficulties arising out of these discussions, these difficulties should be aired with other board members as soon as possible. This stresses again the importance of understanding between the superintendent and members of the Board in a session prior to the establishment of this system of communication. Prevention of misunderstandings is much easier in the area of communications than resolving the differences once they have been established.

Board Communication with the Staff

There are occasions in many Boards of Education throughout the country when individual board members feel the need to communicate directly with individual staff members of the administrative team. Most superintendents have a tendency to discourage this practice. This attitude of the superintendent stems from the basic philosophy that the superintendent communicates with the Board for the staff, and that the Board communicates with the staff through the superintendent. There are some forces, both within education and outside, who are today challenging this basic assumption, but it appears that at this time most superintendents and educational administrators still adhere to this basic philosophy. On certain occasions, however, there are circumstances in which individual board members will communicate directly with individual staff members. Many superintendents are faced with the problem of how to deal effectively with this situation without creating distress on the part of the staff member and without undermining the importance of the individual board members. Sometimes a board member desiring information about a particular subject finds the superintendent unavailable. In this case the board member will often contact directly the staff member who carries this responsibility. The staff member, as a result of careful orientation by his superintendent, is reluctant to communicate directly with the member of the Board of Education. In some circumstances board members do this deliberately in order to get information which they feel has not been given to them by the superintendent. Whatever the reason might be for board members communicating directly with the staff, this appears to be a dangerous practice. Both the superintendent and members of the Board of Education appear to operate in a more reasonable fashion when the philosophy of communication is adhered to that emphasizes the role of the superintendent as both executive officer of the Board and as the intermediate step between the Board and the staff.

Superintendents often wonder how to deal with the board member who does continually contact individual staff members for consultations, opinions, or information. One technique that may help solve the problem is to advise all staff members to listen patiently and to offer appreciation for the problem presented by the board member, and then invite the board member to accompany the staff member to the superintendent's office to present the problem. By this means there is an effort on the part of the staff member to help obtain an answer for the board member and at the same time to avoid the pitfall of arousing the ire of the superintendent for communicating directly with an individual board member. Here again it cannot be stressed too strongly that these problems can be resolved easily when an atmosphere of mutual trust and respect has been established. But it should be clear that the problems can be exceedingly difficult if this atmosphere does not exist.

The superintendent faces a real dilemma in the question of board communication with the staff. He has a real responsibility to inform both the staff and the members of the Board of Education on the desired procedures. In addition he has the responsibility for informing, as to content, the members of the Board and the members of the staff concerning various activities of the school system. He must provide also a framework for effective two-way communication so that staff members and board members may have access to his office for discussion of problems that occur to them.

Orientation of New Members of the Board for Effective Communication

One of the first tasks of a superintendent in the orientation of new members of the Board of Education is to acquaint the new members with the procedures that are used to establish effective communication between the superintendent and the members of the Board. In this orientation period, while the board members are learning about the school system in its entirety, the superintendent should not forget to stress the necessity of effective communication. In this period of time when the board member is just learning the duties of office, he should be made welcome to inquire of the superintendent concerning any aspect of the schools' operation. Most superintendents today have a regular formalized program for the orientation of new board members to the school system, but this orientation must definitely include the opportunity for the board member to initiate questions and problems to the superintendent for his discussion and explanation. The board member often feels reluctant to take too much initiative in the early stages of his service on the Board so the superintendent should be certain that the avenues of communication are explained clearly to the new board member, and he must also take the initiative to insist that these avenues of communication remain open, clear and understandable to the new board member.

The program of orientation for new school board members should include personal visits to the schools within the system. This will depend a great deal on the size of the school system and its complexity, but it is extremely important that new board members have some concept of the physical condition of the school buildings, their location, and a general knowledge of the condition of facilities within the system. As part of this orientation, the superintendent would want to acquaint the new board member with the operations of the central office. The board member should have an understanding of how business is conducted at the superintendent's office, and what general patterns of operation he follows.

The superintendent should spend time with the board member in helping him understand the procedures for communicating concerning regular and special meetings of the Board. The superintendent should explain the composition of the agenda, how the agenda matters are handled, how the staff participates in the meeting, and particularly how the board chairman and superintendent require special communication. The superintendent should be certain that new members of the Board understand the relationship that exists between the superintendent and individual board members in the matter of effective communications.

As the superintendent ascertains the extent of knowledge of the board member about the school system, he should make every effort to provide whatever information is needed by the board member for his complete orientation. In the process of doing this, avenues of communication must be constantly stressed because it is only through effective communication that board members will be properly oriented to their new positions and will be able to function effectively in those positions.

Press Releases

The superintendent of schools, from time to time, issues press releases for the purpose of informing the public of particular activities of the school system. In the issuance of press releases the superintendent should give some concern to informing the Board prior to the press release on those items he considers to be important. Board members do not like to read in the newspaper concerning events about which they had no previous knowledge. This applies to events which may be coming up at the next meeting of the Board, or for that matter, on regular occurrences within the school system. There will be many circumstances in which the superintendent will release information to the press and other media without consultation with members of the Board, but this becomes a matter of judgment for the superintendent. Specific examples of cases in which the superintendent might release information to the public would be on such matters as enrollment figures, change of hours or bus schedules for specific occasions, announcement of special conference dates, and other matters of a routine nature. The superintendent should keep a close eye on this question of communications in relation to those items that appear in the press. If he perceives that board members are learning too many things from the newspapers that were not given to them in prior notification, he should have reason to change his procedures.

Communication with Other Boards and State and National Associations

New problems becoming evident today throughout the country require knowledge of the actions of other organizations. Board members are often desirous of information concerning the actions of other Boards of Education and concerning both attitudes and actions of their state and national associations. Such new problems as negotiations with the staff, bonding limits, and joint purchasing are giving indications of a period of greater cooperation between neighboring Boards of Education and between individual Boards and their state and national associations. The superintendent can be helpful in the establishment of procedures for this communication, where it is possible, and where it is desirous by the Board of Education. Superintendents of neighboring districts can help in this communication. It is often advantageous to members of the Board to learn of the action taken by neighboring Boards on problems of a similar nature to those now under consideration. This appears to be particularly true in times of crisis in the school system. If a teacher walkout or strike is occurring in one school district, the members of Boards of Education in surrounding school districts are bound to be concerned and would like to be informed of the status of the situation. The superintendent and members of the Board must use good judgment in notifying surrounding Boards and administrators of the details and results of the conflict that exists and what steps are being taken to resolve the problem. Many board members and superintendents feel today that they cannot remain isolated within their own districts on particular kinds of problems. They feel, further, that it is absolutely essential that they have the opportunity to communicate with other board members and that they understand the problems of other school districts as these school districts are facing problems of a nature that might become their problems in the near future.

The whole question of communications between the superintendent and the Board of Education is a complex one. Reams of material have been written concerning this question. Many superintendents have different ideas as to the most effective means of communication with the Board of Education. Many board members have ideas as to how this can be most effectively accomplished. There is great variation in different sized school systems and in various parts of the country as to methodology for this effective communication. The superintendent should study these methods now in operation, analyze their results, analyze his own situation very carefully, and then establish some definite procedures for communicating with his Board of Education. In the process of establishing this procedure he should take into account the personalities of the members of the Board, the administrative operational procedures, and the policies of his Board of Education. Having done this, he should then prepare a suggested procedure for discussion with the Board so that all who are concerned in the matter of board administration communication would understand the process, the intent, and be able to analyze the results.

Review of Suggested Procedures

1. Effective Board-superintendent communications is a prime responsibility of the superintendent.
2. An initial meeting of the superintendent and the Board should provide the framework for good communication.
3. The superintendent should establish a regular periodic method for written communication with the Board.
4. He should use a concise, straightforward method of communicating and eliminate educational jargon.
5. The superintendent should be aware of the dangers of personal social contacts with individual board members.
6. The superintendent must establish special communication with the chairman of the Board, but also recognize the dangers of these special communications.
7. The Board and the superintendent together should consider the desirability of arranging methods of communication with other Boards and with their state and national associations.
8. The most important element in effective communication between the superintendent and the Board is an atmosphere of mutual trust, respect and understanding.

EXHIBIT A

BOARD MEMORANDUM NO. 23

February 11, 19___

TO: Members of the School Board

FROM: Jack L. Davidson, Superintendent

RE: REPORT OF THE STATE LEGISLATIVE AUDITOR COVERING THE SCHOOL RECORDS FROM JULY 1 THROUGH JUNE 30, TWO YEARS LATER.

You have each received a copy of the tentative audit report for the two-year period indicated above. A careful study of the items mentioned indicated that a written explanation to the auditor appealing any of their findings would not be appropriate or helpful. The findings of the audit report appear to be factual and fair. Dr. _____ has prepared comments on each of the items mentioned by the auditor. I am enclosing these comments for your consideration. I have been studying the report by _____, _____, and _____, and find some correlation between their recommendations and the findings of the audit report. We are currently looking at possibilities of implementing some of the recommendations of that report. In the meantime, I will appreciate any reaction to the comments on the audit which are enclosed.

RE: PUBLIC HEARINGS ON LOCAL LEGISLATION WITH OUR LEGISLATIVE DELEGATION

I received today a memo from the three members of our legislative delegation setting public hearings in the Manatee County Courthouse for March 1 and March 22. Since the board authorized Mr. _____ to prepare a proposal relating to the suggested change from our minimum purchase amount, it would seem appropriate that this be presented to the delegation at the meeting on March 1st. You will recall that this would change the amount from $500 to $1,000 requiring bids and approval by the board. This would be consistent with current state law. Also, it would be appropriate for us to present any other local legislation which may be desirable. If you have any suggestions along this line I will be happy to receive them and pass them along to Mr. ———— for preparation.

RE: COMMUNITY MENTAL HEALTH PROGRAM FOR MANATEE
      COUNTY

The Manatee-Sarasota Guidance Center is in the process of developing a Community Mental Health Program for Manatee County. I have discussed, with Dr. ———— and Mr. ————, methods by which the school system can benefit directly from the Guidance Center and from the new wing at the hospital dealing with problems of mental health.

There is proposed the addition of one full time psychiatric social worker to the staff of the Guidance Center, whose duties will be visiting each school at appropriate hours to meet informally with teachers and other school personnel to discuss problems on a continuing basis, and to provide a more direct liaison between the Guidance Center and the schools. Covering all the schools would utilize the services of a full time psychiatric social worker.

The Guidance Center is hopeful of obtaining federal funds for this new position. The federal funds would provide 75% of the salary for such a person the first year, escalating downward at the rate of 15% per year over a period of five years. The State Division of Community Mental Health will assist with 50% of the remaining fraction which means that the cost to the school system would be 12½% of the salary and expenses for the person the first year — roughly $1,500 to $2,000.

In discussing this with Dr. ————, I indicated that I was personally very much in favor of the program and felt that we would benefit greatly from a close cooperation with the Guidance Center and from the full time services of a psychiatric social worker. I had intended to have this discussed at our last meeting but found the press of time made this a bit difficult. Consequently, I am bringing the matter to your attention through this memorandum so that you may reflect on the possibilities offered by this program. I would like to write Dr. _____ indicating our support of the program and that formal action to approve the program would be presented at the next regular meeting of the Board. May I ask if you have any objections to this program, that you notify me by Friday, February 21st, if possible, otherwise I will write Dr. _____ of our interest and advise him that formal action can be taken at the regular March meeting. I know that several of you have been interested in the development of our exceptional child programs and our programs of mental health. I have discussed with Mr. _____ _____, Mental Health Coordinator at the Manatee Memorial Hospital, the opportunities for additional kinds of cooperation with the hospital. I believe we are on the right track toward developing a more comprehensive program in the areas of mental health and special education.

RE: COMMUNITY RELATIONS

For some time I have been giving considerable thought to the need of involvement of the citizenry of Manatee County in the activities and programs of the school system. It appears to me to be one of our most pressing needs. In line with this thinking, I have been considering the major areas of concern in which we will be involved in the immediate future. In projecting our long range building needs, the curriculum revisions that might be necessary, the financing of education at the local level, and community involvement, it appears that there are ways we can pursue to involve the citizenry more completely in the plans for the school system for the years ahead. In the near future I hope to have available for you a proposal for the creation of specific advisory committees drawn from the county dealing with the major areas of future concern. It would seem appropriate to me that we think together on the following matters:

1. What are the major areas of concern that require consideration and thoughtful planning?
2. Once these major areas have been determined, what lay citizens from the community could serve on citizen advisory committees?
3. Would it be appropriate to assign a specific staff mem-

ber to serve as a consultant to each advisory committee?

4. The guidelines for the work of the committees should be established so that the committees are involved in fact and in practice rather than simply in theory, or as rubber stamps for any actions we might contemplate. At the same time, those committees should not be capable of taking specific actions but only making recommendations to the administration and the school board for future decisions.

5. It would seem appropriate that the advisory committees should be named by the school board rather than by the superintendent.

I believe if we provide these activities appropriately they can be of tremendous help in planning for the future. Coincidentally, they can also serve as a means of reversing the treatment, which appears to be nationwide, of defeating the majority of major bond issues for school purposes. The major purpose would not be to sell a bond issue but it should prove to be an advantage in future bond issues. I would appreciate your reactions to this proposal whenever you have the opportunity.

RE: SCHOOL REORGANIZATION PLAN

Our proposal, which was adopted by the Board to comply with the court order of Judge ——, has been sent to ——, attorney for the NAACP in Jacksonville. Mr. —— will come to Bradenton some time after the 20th of February to review the plan with us.

May I say at this time that I believe the Board is to be complimented for its stand on this matter in spite of a rather belligerent minority which, as usual, was very outspoken. It was not an easy decision for you to make, yet I think most people realized it was the only sound decision to make. In addition, because of your concerted action, I think the School Board of Manatee County stands a bit taller now as a result of the action.

JLD:md
Enclosure

EXHIBIT B

BOARD MEMORANDUM NO. 27

March 18, 19___

TO: Members of the School Board of Manatee County

FROM: Jack L. Davidson, Superintendent of Schools

SUBJECT: "X" High School Situation

Monday morning nearly 100 Negro students remained in the Cafeteria following their arrival at school rather than going to their regular first period class. They informed Mr. _____ that they were protesting the fact that no Negroes had been selected as cheerleaders in the voting the previous Friday. We immediately sent Mrs. _____, Mr. _____, and Mrs. _____ out to counsel with the students. The students were orderly and peaceful. They stayed in the Cafeteria until time for the lunch period and then moved to the Auditorium where the counseling continued. They presented a list of requests to Mr. _____ and Mr. _____ responded to these about 3 P.M. in the afternoon. Mr. _____ and I were in constant communication throughout the day. I wanted to make certain that sufficient time was given to counseling these students so that, if possible, we could either avert any student protest or at least be in a more defensible position in the event the protest did occur. The student requests were not a consensus of the entire group but were simply statements written by various individual students. The major request was that they be given one Negro cheerleader for the varsity and one Negro cheerleader for the junior varsity team and that they be guaranteed there would be at least one black cheerleader every year in the future. They also suggested a review of the selection procedure. We agreed to a review of the selection procedure and a study of them but, of course, refused to guarantee Negro cheerleaders either now or in the future. I reviewed the selection procedure carefully and it appears that it was handled very fairly. The panel of judges is made up of some faculty members and some students. There were three Negro judges out of approximately 20. Of the 32 students who applied and tried out, only 4 were Negroes. It so happened that none of them were elected. Prior to leaving school Monday afternoon, Mr. _____ informed the students that they would be expected to return to class on Tuesday morning. Monday evening the students held a meeting of their own which was attended by a few adults, including Reverend _____ and Reverend _____ of the NAACP.

This morning, Tuesday, the students assembled outside the school. They were then assembled in the Cafeteria by Mr. _____. After consultation between the two of us, Mr. _____ informed the students that they were to return to class. If they did not return to class they would have to leave the campus and be subject to suspension or other disciplinary action, including the possibility of loss of eligibility for participation in the student activities. The students left in a very orderly fashion. All of their activities to this point have been very orderly and quiet. After leaving the campus they assembled on the road across from the high school and marched up and down. I alerted the Sheriff's Office and the Juvenile Officer to go to "X" High School in plain clothes and unmarked cars to just maintain a surveillance of the situation to make sure it stayed under control and advised Sheriff _____ that our primary purpose was to avoid provoking incidents of any kind. The Sheriff has been very cooperative in carrying this out. Mr. _____ and I, along with Colonel _____ and Mr. _____, met with Reverend _____ and Reverend _____ for over an hour. They wanted us to guarantee a black cheerleader and guarantee black representatives to the Student Council regardless of the elective process.

I have released a notice to the press this afternoon explaining the situation and explaining the fact that those students who left the campus and refused to go to class are suspended from school pending parental conferences. We did not want to fix a set amount of time for the suspension but preferred to keep this flexible so that we might be able to deal with any students who wished to return right away. The students are aware of the fact that they were given an unexcused absence for their inattendance in the class on Monday and were also told what was involved in a suspension from school. In such a suspension the students are given a zero for each class for every day they miss and are not given the opportunity to make up the work. We explained to them, and to Reverend _____ and Reverend _____, that this could be a very serious thing for the students since final examinations for this quarter will be coming up in the near future. At this point this has not impressed particularly either the students or the two representatives of the NAACP. Some of the students have already indicated to Mr. _____ their desire to return to class. He will deal with them on an individual basis and probably allow them to return as they make the request. Most of the leadership for the students seems to come from a few Negro girls.

My intention in the matter has been to allow sufficient time for counseling, discussion and understanding, then to make it clear to the students the implications and ramifications of their action, then to take the action firmly but without a lot of fanfare and with no malice. As we understand it, the students are planning to attempt to get students from "Y" High School and "Z" High School to join in the walkout if their requests are not met. If this should happen, we are making preparations to deal with this problem in the same way. I have no intention of turning over the operation of any high school or the school system to a group of students no matter how large that group might be. Things have a tendency to happen rather quickly in this kind of activity but I will make every effort to keep you informed as we progress. School administration today is not a boring occupation and is not for the fainthearted. Be sure to call me if you have any questions.

JLD:md

3

Planning and Developing the Board Meeting Agenda

The printed agenda for meetings of the Board of Education determines the content and the sequence of important events facing the school system. Planning and developing the agenda is the responsibility primarily of the Superintendent of Schools. The wise superintendent will see to it that this planning is done cooperatively with the Board and with members of his planning team. Some of the important considerations involved in preparing the agenda are discussed in some detail in this chapter.

Establishing a General Format

The superintendent and the Board, together, should adopt a general format which will be followed for all regular meetings of the Board of Education. This format should be general in nature so that all special problems requiring attention may fall somewhere within the broad outline. This serves a dual purpose. Board members and the public will be assured that all meetings will follow some definite plan for order and the superintendent will be aided in his planning of the agenda by having an outline to follow for each regular meeting. Once this is established cooperatively by the Board and the superintendent, it should be followed for each meeting. The superintendent should adhere to the schedule until such time as the Board decides that a change in the format is desirable.

Different school systems will see the need for different kinds of formats depending on the nature of the Board's activities, its involvement in the school system, and the size and complexity of the operation. Following are some examples of general formats that might be utilized.

Order of Business:

1. Call to order — statement of purpose of meeting
2. Roll call of members
3. Approval of minutes from previous meeting
4. Communications and petitions
5. Report from Superintendent of Schools
6. Unfinished business
7. New business
8. Visitor participation

General Agenda for Board Meeting:

1. Call to Order
2. Approval of Minutes
3. Items for Action
4. Items for Information
5. Old Business
6. New Business
7. Adjournment

It should be noted that each system should adopt a general format that will meet the needs that are peculiar to that particular operation. A logical plan by which to accomplish this would be for the superintendent to compile a suggested format and submit it to the board chairman. After they agree, the format should be presented to the total Board. When agreement is reached the new format should be adopted by the Board at a public meeting and released to the press and the general public. This format can be published as part of a board brochure which can be made available to all visitors to the meetings. Such a brochure might take several forms. A number of school systems throughout the country utilize these brochures to good advantage. Some of the topics that might be included in such a brochure include the following:

Date, time, and place of official meetings
Role of the Board of Education

Procedures to address the Board
School-community relations
Your Board of Education
Procedures and activities of the Board
Problem solving procedure for individuals or groups
Listing of the Board of Education members

A brochure of this type has many advantages. It can be distributed at regular meetings, used as part of the public relations program, and be part of a recruiting package for new employees. It has great advantage also in the orientation of new board members.

Special meetings of the Board may or may not follow this general format, depending on the nature of the meeting. In cases where meetings are held to consider only one or two major items, the general format may not be followed. This might apply to special meetings to consider provisions for new buildings, bond resolutions, work session on budgets, etc. The general format should be followed, however, for all regular meetings.

Selection of Items

The selection of items to be included on the agenda is a matter of great importance. The strategic location of items often has a bearing on the success or failure of that item. Materials for consideration by the Board can be categorized by the superintendent into two basic areas:

1. Long range plans
2. Immediate needs

The planning team should concern itself in the planning stage with matters of long range importance as well as with those items requiring immediate attention. One of the first considerations of meetings of the planning team should be the question of long range planning and the long range goals of the school system. This thinking is based on the idea that the immediate needs are generally obvious and always demanding. Certain personnel must be employed, purchases must be made, bills paid, resolutions adopted, and other immediate needs met. If the planning team does not give concentrated attention to long range planning, however, it can be easily neglected. This is the time and the place for long range planning to be brought to the attention of the Board of Education. The person with ultimate responsibility in the various major divisions of the school system should have the responsibility for calling the attention of the team to the necessary long range thinking and planning in that area of concern. During the planning session the superintendent should evaluate the proposed agenda in its entirety to determine those items which reflect the long range needs of the school system. It cannot be emphasized too strongly that the planning team must assume the responsibility for bringing the long range needs of the school system to the attention of the board for consideration, discussion, and ultimate action.

The immediate needs of the school system are dictated by the events of the present. While there are many differences from one system to the other, the immediate concerns of all school systems are quite similar. Almost every school system faces day-to-day problems in instruction, business, administration, buildings and grounds, attendance zones, and personnel, which must be decided by the Board.

Items for the agenda are generally proposed by the planning team and by members of the Board of Education. There are occasions, of course, in which items for the agenda are requested by members of the public or a staff member, but most of the agenda items come from the Board or the planning team. In all cases the superintendent is in a position to make the final decision for the planning team on those items which are to be included in the agenda. Requests of board members for the placement of items on the agenda will be honored almost without exception.

Style of the Agenda

The style used in the makeup of the agenda should be established by the planning team with the approval of the Board and should remain constant from one meeting to the next. The agenda materials, which are compiled, should be arranged in a logical, systematic manner. Board members are lay citizens who are generally involved in occupational interests outside the field of education. It is sometimes difficult for them to be as knowledgeable about school operations as the superintendent would like for them to be. It stands to reason that the materials supporting the agenda should be explanatory, concise, and as complete as possible.

All the materials involved in the agenda for the meeting should be compiled into a folder for each board member and each member of the planning team. The board member's name should be placed on the cover of this hardback binder or folder, along with the date and time of the meeting. This single binder then becomes a permanent file of that meeting for the board member. As the materials are sent to the board members, the superintendent should include a cover memorandum that will clear up any necessary details.

Every item on the agenda requiring any explanation at all should carry with it an explanatory sheet so that board members will have in one concise package a complete explanation of each item. This explanatory sheet should also follow a prescribed pattern. Four items are worthy of consideration:

1. Background Information
2. Administrative Considerations
3. Recommendation
4. Action Required

Examples of a sample agenda and background material for items of the agenda may be found in the Exhibits at the end of this chapter.

The actual techniques of compiling the agenda are important also. In cases where the agenda is somewhat involved and complex, it is all the more important that an effort be made to simplify the agenda through good organization. Once the organization has been established, it is important that careful consideration be given to the typing and duplicating of the agenda and all the supporting materials. If materials are prepared by different departments or divisions within the school system, care should be taken to use typewriters with the same type style. Where this occurs, it is best to have the superintendent's secretary responsible for overseeing the final typing of master copies prior to duplication. This enables the agenda to be presented in a uniform businesslike way. The agenda folders should be either indexed or divided by small tabs for easy reference by the members of the Board. This is particularly true when the agenda is complex and the supporting materials are voluminous.

Placement of Items for the Agenda

The superintendent and the planning team must give careful thought to the placement of items on the agenda. It is generally considered good practice to dispose of most routine items as early in the meeting as possible. While this is not always true, it is a useful general rule. In addition, those items which require action by the Board should be separated from those items which are merely matters of information, and the items for action should occur before the items for information. The attention of the Board can be generally plotted on a curve with reasonably high interest and attention at the beginning of the meeting; the highest concentration during the central part of the meeting; and the least amount toward the end. If routine items for action are handled first, then the items involving long range decisions or unusual events handled next, with items of information coming near the end of the meeting, the Board's attention and concentration can be put to the best use.

Most every Board of Education finds it difficult to devote adequate time to the program of instruction and curriculum. Different Boards approach this problem in different ways. Some designate one special meeting per month just for curriculum and instruction. Others hold periodic meetings for this purpose. In situations where this is not feasible, it is appropriate to designate a certain time in the meeting for special reports. It would seem that perhaps the best time for these special reports would be at the very beginning of the meeting prior to those matters which require action by the Board. If special reports are left until the end of the meeting, they are often not given the attention they deserve or are shortened due to the press of time. Special reports to the Board must be carefully organized and well presented. Background information and material on the subject to be covered should be sent to the Board with all the other agenda materials. The person making the report may then refer to the background material previously provided but should not read from it verbatim. Such reports can be very enlightening to the Board but they should follow a logical sequence. This requires careful planning by the staff member in charge of that particular operation.

Each agenda should carry a time schedule. It should be understood by all concerned that it is not always possible, or even necessary, to adhere religiously to this time schedule. It can be very helpful, however, in moving through the meeting with dispatch. The planning team should make suggestions to the superintendent concerning the amount of time that might be involved in particular subjects. The superintendent in turn should discuss with the chairman the time schedule and particularly any areas which tend to be controversial. If members of the audience are to be involved, the board chairman should have some idea in advance of the amount of time that will be allotted for audience participation on that particular item. Experience is probably the best teacher in the matter of timing items on the agenda. It is very hard to be accurate in predicting the amount of time a Board might spend on a particular item, but placing a time allocation for each major category of the agenda can be extremely helpful to the chairman and to the entire Board. Under no circumstances, however, should the time schedule be adhered to so diligently that it interferes with the successful and thoughtful consideration of important matters before the Board. It will become apparent that less time will be spent by the Board in rambling discussion when adequate background information has been supplied and a time schedule is suggested.

Occasionally a Board of Education must deal with one individual or more who, for one reason or another, consumes more than his share of the time and the attention during the meeting. If the board member is consistent with this kind of behavior it might be well to take this into consideration in determining the time schedule. Unfortunately, this is often true in those months immediately preceding an election. Some superintendents make an allowance for this by assigning an "X" factor to the time schedule simply for the purpose of speech making and appealing to the press. There is no reason to ignore this factor since it is often a question of facing reality. Other board members not up for election are generally tolerant of this situation and the superintendent must understand the motivation and the action of the board member and plan for it. Under no circumstance should the superintendent take any significant action during the meeting to interfere with this process. By so doing he may easily jeopardize both his effectiveness and his own security.

Distribution of Agendas

In order for the Board to study adequately the background material supplied for the meeting, the agendas must be delivered several days prior to the meeting. As discussed in Chapter 1, the agendas should be delivered to the Board before they are released to the press in order to insure that board members will not read about the forthcoming meeting in the press before they have received the material.

The question which often causes difficulty in some school systems is the problem of determining who will receive copies of the agenda and supporting materials. The Board and the superintendent together should decide who will receive these materials. In some cases agendas are sent only to board members. In others, the materials are sent to the PTA Councils, the local education association or union, administrative groups, Chamber of Commerce, and citizens tax groups. This is a determination which must be made locally. The important thing is that this be established by the Board and the superintendent together in order to avoid embarrassing situations. It would be appropriate to send at least the agenda itself to those people in the community who have a particular interest in specific items on the agenda. If a person is to appear before the Board he should have a copy of the agenda in order to know at what point his particular item will be discussed.

In most all communities there is considerable interest in the work of the Board of Education. In some areas various kinds of organizations are especially interested in the work of the Board. In some cases these are pressure groups designed to influence the directions of the school system through the activities of the Board of Education. These organizations will often request of the superintendent advance copies of the agenda and other supporting materials. This is another reason why the Board and the superintendent should determine in advance how the agenda will be distributed. This can serve as a protection both to the Board and the superintendent and avoid possible conflict and embarrassment.

In spite of the great advantages of careful pre-planning and organization for meetings of the Board, there are some dangers involved. If the board has adequate background information and careful research has been done concerning the problem at hand, board members do not generally spend as much time discussing problems as they might have done previously. This is due simply to the fact that most of their questions have been answered by the information sheets provided for them by the staff. The danger in this situation is that it may appear to the audience, or to the press, that action is being taken strictly on the recommendation of the superintendent with very little thought or discussion. Some reporters have a tendency to feel that board meetings become dull and routine as very few spectacular things occur. To offset this situation, the Board and the superintendent should make it clear to the press and the public the kind of information and background material that is being used in arriving at decisions. If, in addition, the press is supplied with virtually the same background information, the chances for misunderstanding are lessened. The great number of advantages of careful and complete planning more than offset the few dangers involved.

Review of Suggested Procedures

1. Establish a general format for all regular meetings of the Board.
2. Select the items for the agenda carefully with an eye toward long range planning as well as meeting the immediate needs of the school system.

3. Establish a consistent style for the agenda.
4. Provide comprehensive background information on each item of the agenda.
5. Compile all the background information into a single folder which will serve as a file for each board member.
6. Consider routine items for action first, then items for information.
7. Establish a time schedule to be used as a guide for the meeting.
8. Determine cooperatively the distribution of the agenda.

EXHIBIT C

AGENDA

X COUNTY BOARD OF EDUCATION
REGULAR MEETING, TUESDAY, JANUARY 7, 19—
9:00 A.M.

9:00   A.M.   I.   CALL TO ORDER

9:00 — 9:10 A.M.   II.   RECOGNITION
            Retiring Board Members and Trustees

9:10 — 9:30 A.M.   III.   REORGANIZATION
      A. Commissions presented by New Board members
      B. Administering Oath of Office — Judge John A. Jones
      C. Election of officers
      D. Change of Name of Board in accordance with Constitutional Change

9:30 — 9:35 A.M.   IV.   APPROVAL OF MINUTES
            November 21, 19— — Special Mtg.
            December 5, 19— — Regular Mtg.

                     V.   ITEMS FOR ACTION
      A. Building and Grounds
9:35 — 9:50 A.M.   1. Approval of final plans for the Z Elementary School
9:55 — 10:00 A.M.   2. Change Order #1 on Phase II of the Area Vocational and Technical Center for addition to contract
10:00 — 10:05 A.M.   3. Renewal of lease for X Action Park, Inc.
10:05 — 10:15 A.M.   4. Report on insurance and authorization for lease to Day Care Center Inc. on use of "Y" School

		B. Bids
10:15 — 10:25 A.M.		1. Routine:
		a. Furniture — classroom
		b. Furniture — office
		c. Stage curtains
		d. Canned foods
		e. Meat products
10:25 — 10:30 A.M.		2. Waiver of Bid Requirement
		a. Electric typewriters
		C. Budget and Finance
10:30 — 10:35 A.M.		1. Final adoption of the 19___-19___ K-12 Budget
		2. Resolution to certify millage to the Tax Assessor and State Superintendent
		3. Monthly Financial Statement — December
		D. Attendance
10:35 — 10:40 A.M.		1. Special attendance requests
		E. Personnel
10:40 — 10:50 A.M.		1. Resignations of instructional and non-instructional personnel
		2. Appointment of instructional and non-instructional personnel
10:50 — 11:05 A.M.	VI.	ITEMS FOR INFORMATION
		A. Reorganization of county-wide staff
		B. Report on school properties
		C. Internal Accounts Report
		D. Leave List
	VII.	OLD BUSINESS
11:05 — 11:20 A.M.		A. Progress report on Tax Sheltered Annuities
	VIII.	NEW BUSINESS
11:20 — 11:30 A.M.		A. Resolution and Agreement with Educational Television
11:30 — 11:45 A.M.		B. Recognition of X Education Association

11:45   A.M.   IX.   ADJOURNMENT

NOTE: This meeting was considered by the Planning Committee to be too lengthy for a special report on curriculum. If a report had been included it would have been the first item on the Agenda.

EXHIBIT D

SUBJECT: EXTENSION OF LEASE TO "X" ACTION PARK, INC.

BACKGROUND INFORMATION:
In December 19___, the School Board gave the "X" Action Park, Inc. a one-year lease on land in the South Y Head Start Center area that was formerly the Experimental Station. This land was to be used by the organization to set up picnic and recreation areas and to permit families desiring to do so to have garden plots. Some progress has been made by the "X" Action Park, Inc. This was outlined to the board in detail at the November meeting along with plans for future action.

ADMINISTRATIVE CONSIDERATION:
At this time there is no other utilization of the land contemplated and it seems to be good human relations to permit the land to be used. The President of "X" Action Park, Inc. works closely with our Assistant Superintendent for Business in a cooperative manner. Obligations are clearly understood. The lease has been approved by the school attorney.

RECOMMENDATION:
That the School Board grant the "X" Action Park, Inc. a one-year extension of the lease on lands adjacent to the South Y Head Start Center as stipulated in the lease.

ACTION REQUIRED:
Board approval on the lease.

EXHIBIT E

TABULATION OF BIDS ON FURNITURE – CLASSROOM   TOTAL – $2440.95

Bids Due: 11 A.M., Wednesday, December 18, 19___

BIDDERS	Item 1. $1383.75 — 225 Chairs Classroom-18"	Item 2. $721.50 — 30 Reading Tables 30" x 72" x 30"	Item 3. $173.82 — 6 Reading Tables 30" x 96" x 30"	Item 4. $161.88 — 6 Reading Tables Adjustable Height
The ABC Company	7.50	33.35 Alt.	41.15 Alt.	47.15
The Green Manufacturing Company	9.55 (4)		70.15 (4)	48.75 (4)
The BCD Seating Company		28.55	33.55	36.20
The Jones-Smith Company	8.40	43.55 Alt.		50.45
Black Manufacturing, Inc.	7.45			
Baker Manufacturing Company	9.85 Alt. (1) 9.55	34.70 Alt. (1) 34.40	38.55 Alt.	41.70 Alt. (1) 41.30 Alt.

	Item 1	Item 2	Item 3	Item 4
The DEF Manufacturing Company	6.23 (2)	29.00 (3)	33.85 (3)	33.26 (2)
The White-Red Seating Company	5.50	24.05	29.00	45.95
The James Manufacturing, Inc.	6.90 Alt.	34.00 Alt.	39.00 Alt.	46.00 Alt.
Dunn Seating Corporation	14.58 Alt. 12.87 Alt.	35.06	47.04	37.36
The Davis Manufacturing Corporation	6.15	63.90 Alt.	73.65 Alt. 34.50	34.50
The FEG Furniture Company	8.55	30.00		
The "XYZ" Manufacturing Company	5.93	24.27	28.97	26.98

COMMITTEE:
Mr. John Jones
Mr. James Smith
Mr. Ray Blue
Mr. Gene Smith
Mr. Charles Brown

NOTES:
(1) With chrome
(2) Items 1 and 4 — All or None
(3) Items 2 and 3 — All or None
(4) F.O.B. Factory

4

Setting the Stage
and Conducting
the Meeting

The necessity of careful pre-planning for meetings of the Board has been established in previous chapters. All of this careful planning is for nought, however, if planning for the actual meeting is neglected. It is essential that the stage be set properly and adequately for the meeting itself. It should be recognized by the superintendent that the public is exposed to the operations and practices of the school system through meetings of the Board. This is particularly true as the press interprets to the public the policies and procedures that are adopted by the Board at the regular meetings. Each practicing superintendent and board member should be aware of the necessity for carrying the pre-planning directly into the meeting proper.

Adequate Preparation

Each participant in the meeting of the Board of Education should make the necessary preparations for the meeting in light of his own particular responsibility and participation in the meeting. The superintendent is charged with the preparation of all materials and the selection of items to be placed on the agenda. While this selection is generally made cooperatively, it falls usually to the superintendent to make the final decision concerning which items of importance will be placed on the agenda.

Many of the other responsibilities of the superintendent have been discussed in previous chapters, but it cannot be emphasized too strongly that the ultimate responsibility for setting the stage for effective meetings rests squarely on the shoulders of the superintendent.

Individual board members have considerable responsibility in setting the stage for board meetings. The first responsibility is to make sure that each board member does his homework. He must study the agenda and the background information that is supplied on each item on the agenda. He should be certain that he is familiar with the background and administrative considerations for each item. If he does not feel that he has sufficient information on any particular matter, he should contact the superintendent and discuss the matter with him directly. He should prepare a list of questions or comments relating to particular matters on the agenda. He should be certain that he has a clear picture of all facets of the problem and that he understands the implications of alternate courses of action. Under no circumstances should a board member attend a meeting without such preparation. Failure to make the necessary preparation for a meeting often causes a board member to be embarrassed when an obvious answer is given to his question. It should be understood, however, that this does not imply eventual agreement by the board member with the proposed action, but it does emphasize the importance of careful preparation.

Any staff member who plans to be a participant in the board meeting must make careful preparation for his part in the meeting. He must know the time and the place on the agenda for his participation. He must be aware particularly of the amount of time he is allotted on the agenda and plan his presentation within these time limits. If the matter under consideration is one that will produce questions or comments by the board members, he should allow time for this in his planning. He should make special preparations to have on hand, and in place prior to the meeting, any audio visual aids, exhibits, or samples that he will use in his presentation. The staff member should not have to leave the room to pick up additional materials when adequate planning could have prevented such a situation. The superintendent, and the staff member, must recognize that a presentation to the Board by the staff member represents a good opportunity for the promotion of particular programs within the school system. Members of the press and the public present at the meeting draw certain impressions concerning the school program from this presentation. Both adequate preparation and good presentations can enhance the understandings of the program by the Board, the press, and the public.

Citizens from the school district who wish to speak on certain items should also prepare for the meeting. It is to the Board's advantage if a procedure can be established whereby citizens can be heard at meetings of the Board. Most school systems agree that presentations representing the feelings of a group of citizens, or an organization, can be made by one spokesman instead of the Board hearing from a series of speakers representing the same group and speaking on the same subject. The press has a responsibility also in preparing for the meetings. Reporters should obtain the necessary background information from the superintendent through the agenda materials supplied to them prior to the meeting. This becomes more difficult when different reporters cover the meeting from time to time, but this emphasizes the importance of supplying the press, in advance of the meeting, with all pertinent background information and material.

Physical Setting

The physical setting in which meetings of the Board of Education occur is extremely important. This is often overlooked or ignored, but the physical setting for the meeting contributes greatly to the kind of meeting held and to the manner in which the meeting is conducted. Whenever possible meetings of the Board should be conducted in a pleasant atmosphere. Pictures concerning the school system and the school board, awards, or certificates of merit won by the Board of the school system, can be displayed appropriately in the board room. Many school systems today, in planning new or remodeled board facilities, are giving special attention to the meeting room and to adjoining spaces for board members. Those adjoining spaces can be used for filing of materials accumulated by board members and may house a professional library for the use of members of the Board.

Careful thought should be given to the seating of board members and the superintendent at the board table. In deciding upon the seating, recognition should be given to the existence of any factions or personality conflicts that exist. It is foolish to ignore such situations and place natural opponents next to each other or seat them in such a way as to encourage their animosities. The superintendent is generally aware of these differences and should try to plan the seating of board members accordingly. It is important that the necessary physical arrangements be made for the press and for those members of the staff who will be attending the meeting either as participants or as spectators. One indication of poor planning is when staff members or other participants in the meeting do not have seats reserved in appropriate places.

A major complaint of many visitors to school board meetings is their inability to hear the discussion taking place by the Board. The sound system in the board room should be checked periodically to make certain that microphones and speaker systems are working properly. Some visitors to board meetings have come to the conclusion that the Board does not wish to be heard and hence the board members must be trying to operate in secret. It follows, also, that members of the audience should have copies of the agenda so they can follow the actions of the Board and the sequence of events. Ventilation and proper temperature are also important items to consider. A meeting room which is overheated does very little to enhance a smoothly operating board meeting. On the contrary, if the temperature of the participants is apt to rise during the meeting, an overheated room only adds to the consternation and the confusion.

Special arrangements must be made for the secretary who is charged with recording the meeting and keeping notes of the actions of the Board for the compilation of the official minutes. The board chairman and the superintendent should be certain that all motions and board actions are recorded accurately. This implies that special consideration must be made so that the secretary is in a good position to observe and to hear the actions of the Board as well as the participation by the audience. A number of Boards find considerable merit in having a short recess part way through the meeting for a cup of coffee and an opportunity to unwind and relax for a few minutes. A short recess can be particularly helpful following the resolution of some very difficult or controversial matter. A recess timed appropriately will give the opportunity for some members of the audience to leave the meeting after their particular concern has been decided.

Atmosphere

The general atmosphere to be found in meetings of the Board of Education is a matter which seems to run in the same general pattern from meeting to meeting for most Boards. Very seldom does a Board project one image for one meeting and an entirely different image at later meetings. It is true that on certain occasions Boards will have different atmospheres in their meetings due to controversial matters or problems on which there may be great difference of opinion. Every board over a period of time does project some kind of general image to the public, and this image is influenced a great deal by the atmosphere that is established for meetings of the Board. This atmosphere can be determined by board members and the superintendent by deciding in advance the most desirable type of situation. Some Boards, the more efficient ones, conduct their meetings in an atmosphere of efficiency and good business. Others find themselves in a constant state of turmoil due either to excessive audience participation or to the poor planning for the meeting. The image of the Board is reflected through public meetings of the Board and it is to the Board's advantage to determine the image it wants to present to the community and to work hard toward the establishment of that image. This is important because of the reputation of the Board that is being established. Some might say that we should not be concerned about a reputation or Board's public image and that actions should be taken based upon conscience and not upon any desire to please the public. This is a difficult point to make completely clear to the public. The board members must be free to vote their own convictions honestly and forthrightly, and be proud to take a stand on difficult items and controversial matters. The general atmosphere in the meeting, however, can at the same time be one of dignity and professionalism. The image projected by the Board becomes extremely important in light of the general attitude of the public toward the operation of the Board and of the entire school system.

It should be clear to an observer of a meeting of the Board of Education that the meeting is being held to conduct important business relating to education. This does not imply, necessarily, a stilted or pretentious atmosphere, but it does indicate the importance the Board must attach to its function and to the purpose of education in that school system. A visitor to the board meeting should also be impressed with the efficiency of the Board and the atmosphere in which it operates.

One of the most important elements concerning the atmosphere in which the Board operates is one of friendliness and openness. Personality conflicts between board members, or between a board member and the superintendent, must be resolved outside of these meetings if at all possible. Personal animosity at the board level can virtually tear a school system apart. Animosity displayed at meetings of the Board of Education between individual board members and the superintendent can create havoc among the staff members within the system. Members of the staff begin to question where their loyalties must lie in the event of a conflict between the superintendent and an individual board member. Factions among members of the Board sometimes develop and become clear to the community. This generally has a deleterious effect on the school system. Facing reality, however, these cannot always be avoided. It is in such circumstances that the chairman of the Board has a particularly important function to perform. The chairman might appeal to the board members involved to keep the matter under discussion on a professional basis and not allow the discussion to become personalized. He might offer the opportunity for a conference between the board members following the meeting to discuss the matter. If the situation gets extremely touchy, he might declare a short recess in order to allow time for the cooling off of tempers and for a return to a professional atmosphere in the meeting. The chairman should make every effort to resolve these difficulties whenever possible. If the chairman is involved in the personality clash, a neutral member of the Board should attempt to resolve the problem. This is not an easy thing to do. Personality differences are extremely difficult to resolve, but the Board and the school system both suffer if these differences are aired consistently before the public in meetings of the Board. By all means the superintendent should avoid taking sides in these matters. He can perhaps be a peacemaker in private but he must avoid, at all costs, siding with one person or another. He can encourage the resolution of differences between board members but should be extremely careful in the part he actually plays. It should be easily recognized that in situations where the Board is in conflict, the superintendent and his staff can rarely be effective. The foregoing statements in no way are meant to suggest that board members will always agree or vote unanimously. In this day of conflict and indecision, it is difficult to imagine a situation in which board members would always be in agreement. Unanimous decisions on controversial items cannot always be expected. It is important, however, that discussion, debate, and differences of opinion be expressed in a professional, dignified and logical manner. If the Board conducts itself otherwise it can expect a reputation within the community of something less than that which is desirable.

The impression that most every Board would like to leave in the community is that the Board is dedicated to good education with the welfare of individual students always in mind. Individuals representing different interests and prejudices come together as a Board of Education, to resolve problems of the school system and establish directions and policies for the operation of that system.

The Chairman

The chairman has perhaps the key role in the operation of the total meeting. He sets the directions, serves as moderator, establishes the limits for discussion, and plays the key role in setting the tone for the meeting. He must determine who speaks first on various issues presented to the Board, and must take special precautions to show fairness and impartiality to all members of the Board. Certainly he must possess a sense of humor and wit. Most meetings of Boards of Education are too stuffy and too stilted. Exceptions occur, of course. When pressure groups arrive to debate highly controversial matters, the room can be filled with excitement. Many times seemingly routine matters become charged with sparks of electricity. It is in these circumstances that the talents of the chairman are taxed to the limit. Every Board faces meetings in which difficult subjects must be considered. Every Board faces times of crisis, of confusion, and of some disagreement. Every Board faces periods of controversy between the Board and certain groups of citizens. This is a part of the fact of life today. If this kind of an operational procedure becomes routine or normal for a Board of Education, that Board should certainly strive for ways to change the status quo. No Board can do its job if it is operating consistently in a state of emotional duress and turmoil. There is a middle ground between complete dullness and absolute turmoil and chaos. The chairman has a great responsibility in helping to maintain the desired levels of participation. Deciding which person to recognize and how long he should speak becomes a very difficult decision to make when the room is crowded with people anxious to make a presentation. Maintaining an atmosphere of calm and decorum in the midst of heated controversy is not a simple task, but it is one to which the chairman must give his diligent attention.

The chairman has a particular problem whenever he has a fellow board member who decides to play the role of the "star player." Whether this board member chooses this role because he is running for re-election, or because of a simple desire to be well publicized, is important to the chairman. The chairman should try to understand what motivates the board member to act in that particular fashion. An understanding of the motivation can be helpful in dealing with the problem board member. This is not always possible but it is generally worth the effort. Sometimes the best thing that can be done is to hold a conference between the board chairman and the "star player" to discuss the situation and try to come to a logical understanding. If this is not possible, it might be worthwhile for the total Board to meet in an executive session to discuss the situation and try to find a way to manage the problem.

The chairman is charged also with conducting the meeting with dispatch. He should be able to recognize the appropriate time to terminate a discussion and call for the vote on that question. Above all, the chairman must use good judgment in assessing the total situation and the atmosphere of the meeting.

Dealing with Citizens and Groups

Though generally open to the public, the board meetings are not held for the direct benefit of the audience. This is not always understood. There is heard often in various parts of the country a great hue and cry to get people out to attend meetings of the school Board. While an interested citizenry is extremely important to the welfare of a good school system, it is not always desirable to have large crowds of people attending meetings of the Board. Board members are elected, or appointed, to represent the citizens of the community in matters of education. Business of the school system should be conducted in the open where members of the community can attend whenever possible. People who have opinions to express on certain matters of concern generally will do so, either to the board member directly or at meetings of the Board. It is desirable to make citizens welcome at meetings of the Board and to see that they are provided information concerning the conduct of the meeting. The wise Board will make certain that procedures are established for dealing with groups of people in the board meetings prior to the time when these groups appear. Meetings are held to conduct school business and establish policies. Nevertheless, provision should be made for the audience to speak and procedures established whereby items may be placed on the agenda by any citizen applying to the superintendent or board chairman. It is well for the Board to establish an atmosphere in which citizens can be heard attentively and with respect. Board members should avoid, whenever possible, displaying an attitude of antagonism and disrespect. The Board should constantly keep in mind the importance of the subject being discussed and its implications for the students of the school system. This is particularly important in heated discussions of highly controversial matters. This is the time to "keep your cool." It is a time to be certain of your preparation. If you don't know, make no comments and give no promises. It is easy to arrange a time at which a decision could be made in the future. But don't put the matter off indefinitely. Procrastination will anger a group almost as much as decisions which are made too rapidly or without complete information.

The Board of Education represents one of the most important activities in the entire community. It provides policies for the education of the public's most precious possession. Attention given to the atmosphere of the public meetings in which the Board operates is essential for the conduct of effective and productive meetings of the Board. Such meetings enhance the effectiveness of the school system and go a long way toward providing quality education for the students.

Review of Suggested Procedures

1. Remember the necessity for adequate preparation by superintendent, board members, staff members, press and citizens. Do your homework.
2. Provide an adequate setting for the meeting. Give attention to details of seating arrangements, acoustics, ventilation, etc.
3. Provide a competent secretary for recording minutes and a tape recorder for the use of the Board.
4. Discuss the atmosphere best suited to your Board and the image you wish to project.
5. Look for opportunities for good humor and wit.
6. Establish a procedure for dealing with groups and organizations appearing before the Board.
7. Remember that your primary responsibility concerns the welfare of the students within the school system.

5

Action Patterns
for the Superintendent

Not all school Boards operate in the same manner. In the same vein no two superintendents operate alike. Personalities and capabilities of superintendents enter into the matter of the role the superintendent plays during meetings of the Board of Education. The urban superintendent operates in a completely different context from that of the superintendent in the small city. The superintendent of a county system must perform his duties in a different context from that of the superintendent of a small town or small community. Tradition handed down through the years often dictates action patterns for the superintendent, but this is true more in the public life of the superintendent than it is during meetings of the Board. There are so many variables concerning the action of the superintendent in meetings of the Board that it is impossible to establish any pattern of action for him. Certain things are true however, in most cases, that can establish the leadership role of the superintendent. As far as the school system and the community are concerned, the superintendent is on center stage most of the time. It is part of the role he plays as head of one of the largest businesses in the area. At no time does the superintendent seem to be on the spot or in the limelight any more than at meetings of the Board of Education. This being the case, it is important for the practicing superintendent to give attention to his own action patterns during meetings of the Board. Several characteristics are bound to appear during meetings of the Board which reflect both the attitude and the philosophy of the superintendent. Some of these general characteristics, situations, and duties are discussed in this chapter.

Provide Information

One of the chief functions of the superintendent is to provide information for members of the Board so that decisions which must be made by the Board can be made intelligently. The superintendent must be certain that the information he provides is accurate to the best of his ability. He must be certain that it is presented in a concise, clear, and straightforward manner so there is little doubt as to what the information means. The superintendent should remember that he is communicating with laymen as members of his Board of Education. While they generally have more information concerning the school system and a deeper insight into the problems of schools than the average citizen, they are not specialists in the field of education or school administration. They are often individuals with their own professions or business interests, and they sometimes have difficulty following communications that are full of educational jargon and phrases that school administrators are guilty of using with great rapidity. The superintendent should make every effort to present factual matters as graphically as possible. Use charts, graphs and illustrations, if they present the information in a manner that will make the information better understood. It is important to remember also that board members will be using this information for future reference, so all such illustrations should be titled and dated.

If the superintendent, for example, is outlining a new program in vocational education, and uses in his presentation facts and figures relating to the job needs in the community in a particular vocation, the survey of such job needs should be presented clearly and accurately. The material must be authentic. The references for the material should be cited. If a survey was used to assemble the material, this should be noted and the individual completing the survey should be credited for his work. He should also be held responsible for the results of his work. If, in this vocational program, the cooperation of participating businessmen may be required, these businessmen should be identified with a statement as to their willingness to participate. If additional back-up information is available concerning job needs on a state-wide level, this information should be supplied as supplementary information.

The Board should learn very early in the administrative tenure of the superintendent that it can rely on information presented by the superintendent. The Board should also learn that the information will be honestly portrayed whether or not it happens to support a previously established position of either the superintendent or members of the Board. The superintendent must be certain that those staff members who provide him with information on certain areas of concern are competent and thorough. Nothing can weaken the position of the superintendent any faster than information presented to the Board and made public which turns out to be either partially or completely inaccurate or misleading. Where the superintendent must rely on staff members for information, he should make certain that the information is sound and factual before presenting it to the Board. If a survey is made in the school system to determine the number of children who eat breakfast before coming to school, the superintendent would need some means of authenticating the results before presentation to the Board and the public. If a survey is made of the number of children living in a certain neighborhood, the superintendent must be certain that the procedures used to gain this information are realistic and that the count is as accurate as possible. If the superintendent is proposing to the Board a new program in science education, he should be certain that his figures on the cost of laboratory equipment and supplies are as accurate as possible. This cannot be accomplished unless sufficient time and planning are given to the project. The superintendent should be hesitant to present anything to the Board as a result of a crash movement or program wherein sufficient time has not been allotted for planning, research and documentation. There is a great temptation to do this today, particularly in the area of federal programs. So many times the information concerning applications for federally funded programs arrives in the school system with a due date only a short time in the future. The superintendent, in an effort to comply with the established deadline, can possibly succumb to the deadline pressure and submit the program to the Board before he is completely prepared. In the long run this is a foolish procedure. In most instances the school system is not in a position to lose the available federal funds and very rarely would the superintendent advocate this. On the other hand, the superintendent wants to make certain that adequate planning has occurred and that he understands the scope of the program before submitting such an application to the proper authorities. There are times, also, when a request from the State Department of Education requires reports or other information to be delivered in a short space of time. While it is recognized that such emergencies do occur from time to time, the superintendent should be careful that all proposals and reports coming before the Board of Education have been carefully scrutinized prior to presentation to the Board. Six months after the board presentation, when a serious error is found in the material, not many people will remember that there was a short deadline date at the time of application and preparation. This is not an easy matter for the superintendent to combat, because he generally is very interested in meeting all necessary deadline dates. Nevertheless, it is extremely important that the superintendent bear in mind the necessity of verifying all information presented to the Board of Education. In short, the superintendent lays his reputation on the line when he provides information to the Board of Education for consideration. He should do everything in his power to make sure that the information is correct.

Making Recommendations

Information that is provided for the Board can usually produce alternative courses of action. It is a responsibility of the superintendent to either make a definite recommendation to the Board for action or to provide alternative courses of action from which the Board may choose. There is considerable debate among superintendents about this question. Some superintendents refrain from making recommendations on major items, leaving the matter entirely to the Board's discretion. It is the author's own opinion, however, that the leadership position of the superintendency requires that he make a recommendation to the Board on every item of importance facing the Board. His recommendations may take the form of a specific course of action or he may provide alternatives with the recommendation that the Board choose between the alternatives. If a superintendent merely presents the problem to the Board with no suggestion for dealing with the problem, he abdicates his position of leadership and responsibility and hides behind the Board of Education. This does little to enhance the effectiveness of the superintendent. The Board has employed the superintendent as its executive officer and looks to him for leadership as well as for administrative organization and responsibility. The Board has a right to expect its superintendent to take a stand on these matters coming before the board. Board members should understand, of course, that when the superintendent assumes such a stance, he does so at the risk of generating considerable opposition as well as some support. Opposition has a way of making itself known, whereas support is often not quite as verbal and certainly not as outspoken. If the superintendent is willing to exercise his responsibility in making definite recommendations to the Board, the Board should recognize its responsibility in dealing with attacks on the superintendent that result from his stand on a matter. Whereas the Board has a responsibility to insulate the superintendent from unnecessary and unjust public criticism, the superintendent has the responsibility to perform his leadership role and to act decisively and with dispatch. He cannot do this if he sidesteps the issue and fails to present some kind of recommendation on every major issue. In the current situation in public school administration where conflict and dissension are the order of the day, the Board and the superintendent have an obligation to each other. The superintendent should provide leadership for the Board, while the Board in turn must understand and appreciate the role the superintendent plays in making recommendations to the Board.

The Board has the alternative of accepting the recommendation or rejecting it. It should be understood by the superintendent that not all recommendations will be adopted, nor should they be. If the Board adopted every recommendation made by the superintendent it would appear obvious that the Board is not performing its function entirely. On the other hand, if the superintendent finds that the Board is constantly refusing the recommendations of the superintendent, this should be cause for real concern on the part of the superintendent and the Board. Such a situation may indicate a loss of confidence in the ability of the superintendent or it may simply indicate a lack of communication between the superintendent and the Board. There are also many other reasons why the Board may consistently vote against the recommendations of the superintendent, but if this occurs with any kind of frequency or regularity, the superintendent as well as the board members should take the matter under very careful consideration. The superintendent could not be expected to continue to advance firmly his recommendations and ideas if he is consistently thwarted by his Board of Education. The public will sense immediately a lack of confidence by the Board in the superintendent, and will begin to have its own doubts about the abilities and recommendations of the superintendent. In this situation the superintendent should consult first with his planning team in an effort to determine the reasons behind the failures of his recommendations. He should do some real soul searching at this point. Is it because of his lack of information, lack of knowledge, poor presentation, poor planning, or lack of support? On the other hand, is the attitude of the Board simply belligerant, is the Board attempting to show its power, its individuality, or its own initiative? Insofar as is possible, the reasons should be diagnosed and some form of action taken to correct the situation. By all means the superintendent should sit down with the Board and discuss the situation openly and frankly, and then attempt to discern the reasons behind the frequent failure of his recommendations.

Determining the recommendation to make on specific major issues within the school system is a definite responsibility for the superintendent. It should be emphasized here again that the superintendent should not shirk this responsibility. He is in a leadership role and the school system will suffer if that leadership role is not carried out by a professional person. The superintendent must carefully consider all factors before establishing his position on an issue. He should not vacillate from one position to another, and he must be sure to base his recommendations on facts and figures rather than on emotion or fancy. It is helpful if the superintendent can present his recommendation to the Board in a written form that could be the basis for a motion by a member of the Board. It is not necessary that the board member use this form but it should be available should anyone desire to use it. This particular technique is often helpful to board members who have difficulty expressing thoughts in the precise manner they desire. The superintendent will, of course, be aware that once he takes a position on a major issue, the forces of opposition will gather and he may always expect that the opposing forces will be heard and that the battle lines will be drawn on most major issues.

Hardly any issue of significance in today's school operation can be expected to achieve unanimous public support. Opposition and conflict are part of the world in which the superintendent and the Board operate. The prepared superintendent will analyze, prior to the action, the probable opposition and plan ways to deal with that opposition. If the superintendent is facing a question dealing with racial integration, he should attempt to identify where the opposition and the support for his program will exist. If he is dealing with a problem of student activism, he must be ready to face those who feel that students should have a greater voice in the operation of the schools as well as those who feel that students should be seen and not heard. In this particular situation the superintendent's action in the first case of student activism will lay the groundwork for his future decisions dealing with similar problems. If the school system is proposing the adoption of a new program in sex education, for example, the superintendent would certainly want to be able to identify his expected opposition. He should gather together sufficient background material to support the educational stand he will take in that matter. In short, the superintendent must anticipate opposition on most matters being presented to the Board, analyze that opposition, and be prepared to meet it. This is the world in which he lives.

Be Organized

One of the most important factors for a superintendent to consider during a meeting of the Board is his own organization. He should review the agenda carefully; he should be able to anticipate the kinds of questions and comments that are likely to be raised about the issue. He should know his board members well enough to anticipate at least some of their comments and questions, and have some notion of what their attitudes might be on particular matters. The superintendent should strive to leave the impression that he knows where all of the information is that he will need. He should not have large stacks of papers and folders scattered around his place at the board table. If the agenda is voluminous, covering a variety of topics, he should place those items within a notebook or folder and have them tabbed for easy index and reference. He should spend the necessary time before the meeting planning his presentations and reactions so that he knows right where his materials are located, and can be decisive in his actions and in his manner. If the superintendent is not an organized person, he should get the assistance of someone else in the preparation of his material so that at least he does not give the impression of being disorganized. The superintendent should do this or learn to be organized, and the latter is of course preferable. The superintendent should not be in doubt at meeting time as to either his material, his presentation, or his recommendations. His materials should be arranged in the order of use, properly indexed, and the superintendent should have available whatever other helps and aids he might need. Visual aids are often helpful to the superintendent in presenting material to the Board. It is generally better if the superintendent arranges for another staff member to operate the projectors or other audio visual equipment, rather than conducting the operation of the equipment himself. This leaves him free to explain more completely the information contained in the presentation. This requires careful coordination between the superintendent and his staff member. It looks pretty bad for the superintendent to be ready to use some form of visual aid only to find that a bulb has burned out, or the extension cord is not long enough, or the projection is on upside down. One cannot help but wonder about the preparation and organization of the superintendent when this happens. A dress rehersal of such a presentation is certainly in order. In planning the presentation of a particular matter, the superintendent, together with members of his planning team, should spend some time anticipating what the questions, comments, and objections to the proposal might be. Having done this, the superintendent can then prepare answers to these objections. If the superintendent uses a notebook or similar means of compiling all of the information necessary for the meeting for his own use, and studies this material carefully prior to the meeting, he can generally maintain his composure and fight whatever matters he needs to with various groups or individuals.

Nothing detracts more from the image of the superintendent than lack of organization and preparation. If the superintendent is not well organized for meetings of his Board, many people can rightfully assume that he is probably not well organized for the administration of the school system. The superintendent should remember that much of his administration will be mirrored through meetings of the Board of Education and will be interpreted to the public by the press present at the meeting. An occasional lapse followed by a good humored explanation on the part of the superintendent can be accepted by anyone, but the image he projects to the Board and the community at public meetings should be one of a well prepared, well organized, efficient administrator, who knows what he is doing, has the information available when he needs it, and can authenticate his information and recommendations.

The Superintendent Is a Generalist

In thinking about action patterns for the superintendent during meetings for the Board, it becomes clear that the superintendent in today's school system is more of a generalist all the time. He is not a specialist in curriculum or finance, or transportation, or any one of the myriad of areas involved in the operation of a complex school system. While he may have to be well versed in all of these areas, he generally will have someone in the system who is a specialist in each of these various areas. In an extremely small school system where the superintendent carries the responsibility for all of these areas, it is sometimes difficult to follow this same philosophy, but generally speaking, even in those situations, the superintendent is more of a generalist than he is a specialist. This would appear to have real implications for the superintendent during meetings of the Board. The superintendent must decide whether he will make presentations to the Board on areas of special interest, or whether he will call upon a staff member in that area to make the presentation. Some superintendents work at this problem by making a general presentation concerning the subject at hand, then introducing his staff member for the details and specifics of the subject matter. The superintendent, even in the smallest of school systems, must accept the fact that he cannot know *all* about *everything* in his school system. In spite of that assumption, however, it behooves the superintendent to know as much as he can about a particular item before it appears on the agenda for the meeting. There is a point of delineation that must be made by the superintendent between knowing all that you can about a matter and the amount of available time prior to the meeting. Time is a factor and so is capacity for retention. Both of these factors help determine the extent to which the superintendent becomes more of a specialist and less of a generalist.

Every superintendent is faced with the problem of presenting the annual operating budget. Very few items require so much thorough preparation and accountability as the annual budget. This is one area in which the superintendent must be extremely well prepared. He must have available precise information concerning sources of revenue, expected incomes, balances, and anticipated expenses. He cannot be such a specialist, however, that he knows every single detail concerning all facets of the budget. This is a time when the staff member in charge of finance or budgeting can be of great assistance to the superintendent. If a source of state revenue requires detailed explanation, the superintendent should have his assistant in that area prepared to make the necessary explanations. While the superintendent is still a generalist, he has enough special knowledge that he is able to interpret to the Board the budget and all of its operational details. To use another example, if the school system is planning a new program in Science, such as the introduction of a course in Harvard Project Physics, he should be acquainted with the general features of the program and present a summary of the desired program to the Board. If it is desirable to provide detailed information concerning this approach to the study of Physics, a science supervisor, or other person knowledgeable in the subject matter, could be helpful in detailing the course content and philosophy. The superintendent should not be expected by the Board to be a detail man in all levels of the school operation. He must be provided with staff members for this purpose. On the other hand, he can be expected to have sufficient general knowledge of the entire school operation that he can be accountable to the Board for the school programs.

In the preparation of items for the agenda, the superintendent must be certain that members of his staff have been involved in the planning of the item and that he knows their views. As a question is presented to the Board by the superintendent, or by a member of his staff, the viewpoint of the staff member will become clear. His opinions, his ideas, his prejudices, concerning the particular topic under consideration cannot be easily hidden. The superintendent must know prior to the board meeting the feelings of his staff on that particular matter. All things considered, the superintendent in the board meetings is a generalist, but a generalist who is well informed on all items appearing before the Board. While he may not have committed to memory all bits of information necessary for the item under consideration, he will have information readily available and at his fingertips. He will be organized.

Help the Chairman and Other Members

One of the key responsibilities of the superintendent during the meeting is to assist the chairman whenever possible and whenever assistance is needed. This is true particularly of those board members who may be inexperienced in operating and conducting meetings and those who are inexperienced in dealing with pressure groups and irate citizens. It is an area in which the superintendent can be very helpful to the chairman.

On many occasions today the Board will be required to deal with groups of people who are unhappy with the intended action of the Board. It might be a group of parents protesting the change of school district attendance boundaries. It might be representatives of the teacher organization who are dissatisfied with the current approach to professional negotiations or collective bargaining. It might be representation from a group of dissatisfied students and/or their parents. If correct procedures are followed, the Board should be notified prior to the meeting that these groups will appear to present their case. Occasionally, however, emergency situations develop at the last minute prior to the meeting and individuals or groups come to the meeting to be heard. The manner with which the Board deals with these groups of people is extremely important. It is easy to establish a precedent of reacting to pressure. If a group appears before the Board on some particular measure demanding immediate action, and the Board succumbs to the group, the Board can expect a repetition of pressure groups in other circumstances in the future. Success breeds success. The next time a group of citizens becomes dissatisfied with a particular situation, they too can arrive at the board meeting en masse to offer their protest and their suggested solutions. Very rarely should the Board react to any pressure group with action of any kind without having had the opportunity to study the matter and consult with the superintendent. The more desirable procedure is to have the matter presented on the agenda for full consideration. If for some reason this does not, or cannot happen, the Board should take the matter under advisement and offer the opportunity for a decision in the near future. The superintendent can be helpful to the chairman in such matters if he can advise the chairman to arrange a meeting in the future to dispose of the matter, or at the very least a caucus of the board in order to give time for careful consideration. Establishing a precedent by quick reaction to pressure groups can cause the superintendent untold amounts of administrative problems and the Board real concern over the development of future policies.

The superintendent can enhance the effectiveness of the board meeting by offering a suggestion or an idea at an appropriate time. Most suggestions made to the chairman should be made prior to the meeting. The superintendent should avoid, at all costs, embarrassing the chairman and should try to keep him from getting in a position where he may be embarrassed. The superintendent should, of course, discuss the agenda with the chairman prior to the meeting and answer any questions the chairman might have relative to the meeting. In many situations the superintendent and the chairman are physically seated next to each other at the board table so the superintendent can be of assistance to the chairman whenever the chairman so desires.

The superintendent should be careful that he communicates with *all* board members. Don't leave any out. Nothing upsets a board member much more than to find out that other board members have received information from the superintendent that he does not possess. This can easily cause the board member to become suspicious of the superintendent and of his fellow board members. If a board member is out of town prior to the meeting, every effort should be made to communicate with him about the particular problem before the meeting begins. If it is impossible for the super-intendent to do this, he should assign some staff member this responsibility. Such ommissions as this can be the cause of real conflict between the superintendent and members of the Board, even though the intentions of the superintendent were honorable throughout.

General Considerations

The superintendency today requires individuals who are both secure in their positions and willing to exercise the leadership which is required of them. This is often a difficult and lonely role to play. The superintendent knows that in all matters of controversy there will be at least some opposition and dissent. The degree of this opposition and dissent varies from one situation to another but it is present in some form in almost every situation. In today's school situation this opposition can come from members of the citizenry, pressure groups, and irate parents. This has been the case for many years. In addition, however, opposition today may come from members of the staff or from students, or from both. In preparing recommendations for the Board the superintendent must recognize and identify the potential opposition and should notify the Board of this probable opposition whenever he can.

The superintendent, and today's board member as well, must expect criticism and conflict. As a public school administrator the superintendent cannot afford to wear his heart on his sleeve. He must develop, as many people have admonished him to do, a tough hide. To go with this tough hide he has to maintain an open mind and be willing to go the extra mile to resolve controversies which arise in the school system. In short, today's superintendent must be willing to take a stand based upon the best information he can assemble and take that stand with firm conviction and determination. He must not hide behind the Board of Education nor should he attempt to be a solo performer. His role is one of leadership and he can exert this leadership best during meetings of the Board when he has the necessary information; when he is well organized; and when he recognizes his own role as well as the role of the Board.

Review of Suggested Procedures

1. Be sure of your information. Make certain it is reliable and that you can authenticate it if necessary.
2. The superintendent should make a recommendation to the Board on every major issue facing the school system.
3. Be well organized during the board meeting; know where your information is and be able to use it.
4. Remember that the superintendent is a generalist; take advantage of the specialists on your staff.
5. Help the chairman through the difficult spots whenever you can.
6. It takes courage to present your convictions but if they are well founded in fact, your chances of success are much better.

6

Working Cooperatively
with the Press
and Other Media

School systems today need a well informed public. Citizens are more deeply interested in the educational activities of the public schools than at any time in our history. There are many reasons for this. The important role played by education today and the future welfare of our country and its citizens is emphasized constantly through many sources. Education is spending a greater share of the public money. Bond issues and millage elections are becoming increasingly difficult to pass for a variety of reasons. Changes in educational organization and instructional methodology tend to add confusion and lack of understanding to the already troubled picture of public involvement in education. It is small wonder, in the face of these and other circumstances, that school systems have become increasingly concerned about the relationship that exists between the schools and various segments of the public. There is a definite need for greater understanding by the public of the role the schools play in today's society. There is a greater need for knowledge about the school system, its aims and ambitions, its successes and its failures. The community is vitally interested in what happens in the public schools.

Members of the Board of Education represent the community in school affairs. The actions of the Board of Education must be interpreted correctly to the public if the school program is to be understood and supported by the citizenry. Special considerations for the press and other media are a matter of concern to both the Board and the superintendent, but the superintendent carries the chief responsibility of informing all public information agencies of the activities of the school system. If representatives of the press and other media are not informed completely of the details concerning actions of the Board of Education, the resulting coverage may be either inaccurate or, at the very least, misleading.

Identifying the Roles of Each Party

One of the first ingredients for a successful relationship between the superintendent as a representative of the school system, and the media, is the establishment of a mutual understanding of the roles and responsibilities of each party. The superintendent is charged by the Board of Education with the administration of the school system. The newspaper media and radio, and television announcers, are responsible for the dissemination of news as well as editorial commentary. The superintendent must understand that reporters and editors do not become, automatically, supporters of the superintendent or of the school system. Their job is to report the news. Many reporters are anxious to support the schools, and/or the superintendent, but reporting the news is their major responsibility and they are indoctrinated with the necessity of objective reporting throughout their training and experience. When the superintendent realizes this fact, and accepts the primary role of the media, he can deal more realistically with the problems of communication. The wise superintendent will take the initiative to establish the proper relationship with the media and will work to effect an understanding of the attitude the reporter takes toward his responsibility as a public information representative. The superintendent should be on a first name basis with those who report the school news and with the editor, publisher, or station manager, whenever possible. This is a responsibility primarily of the superintendent. By the same token, however, representatives of the media have a mutual responsibility in knowing and understanding the superintendent of schools and the part he plays in the administration of public education in that community. The superintendent cannot expect that the media officials will automatically sing the praises of the superintendent, the Board of Education, or the school system. This can happen only if reporters are fully informed of the activities of the school system, including both its successful operations and its failures.

It is advisable for the new superintendent to arrange a conference with those reporters who will cover activities of the Board of Education on a regular basis. This is a good time to clarify the role of the superintendent and the role of the reporter. This conference should come at the initiative of the superintendent. The superintendent and the reporters can discuss procedures that will be followed in providing the best possible news coverage for the citizens of the community. They should discuss at this time problems arising from deadline dates, release of materials, and how the superintendent and the reporters will proceed on stories that are uncovered by one newspaper and not known to the others. This is a particularly important point where more than one newspaper or television station competes for news of the school system. It is important also to clarify with the reporters the best time of day to release information. This has a definite bearing on the situation in the case where some of the newspapers are published in the morning and some are afternoon editions. The superintendent should discuss with the reporters the procedures he would plan to follow in relation to press conferences when all members of the press are invited. He should discuss also the procedures to be followed when one newspaper is working on a story which is not being pursued by the others. At this conference the superintendent should give particular attention to covering meetings of the Board of Education. He should ascertain the needs of the press and see what can be done to accommodate them. This should not be construed as a concession to the press or as a means of working to gain their favor. It should be viewed as a recognition of the two-way street of communication and of working together to effect good reporting of school events to the public. If the superintendent did not do this when he first arrived in the community, perhaps it would still be an appropriate thing to do at this time.

The Public Information Specialist

More and more school systems today are recognizing the need for a person who devotes full time in working with public information and community relations. This person is given many titles by various school systems throughout the country but most superintendents recognize the value of such a position. The National School Public Relations Association strongly encourages this position and even helps locate qualified people for school systems. The staff member charged with public relations has an extremely important job in relating the school system to the community it serves. When a school system employs a person in this capacity, it should be understood that he represents the superintendent as the chief administrative officer of the school system. It should be understood at the same time that this staff member is not a press agent for the superintendent. His primary function is to assist the school system in interpreting its programs to the people of the community. The public information officer should act as a door between the school system and the media, not as a wall. They are support personnel. The staff member charged with school-community relations is the school's link with the press and the media. As such, he is the school's front man. He takes responsibility for all of the school system's publications and expedites the work of various groups working with the school system. He can be an extremely valuable person in communicating with the media the activities of the Board of Education. It should be clearly understood, however, that the superintendent still bears the major responsibility for school-community relations. The fact is that with the rising complexity of school administration, the task of school-community relations becomes greater, hence it is appropriate for the superintendent to delegate this responsibility to another staff member. When the school system employs a specialist in this area, the superintendent must be certain that he understands the thinking of this specialist and that the views of the staff member and the superintendent are compatible. Many of the public information specialists have had previous experience in the newspaper field. Many have come from educational backgrounds with only limited experience with the press. It is often difficult for a superintendent to decide whether to employ a previous newspaper man with little knowledge of education, or to employ an educator with little knowledge of the workings of the press. Competent personnel with experience in both fields are hard to find. The purpose in emphasizing this point is to illustrate the importance of the superintendent's selection of this staff member who will be working directly with representatives of the media. The superintendent will do well to give great care to the selection of this person.

Background Information for the Media

Most newspapers, and other media, assign regular reporters to cover educational matters for the school system. Many of the education editors and writers are extremely well informed and knowledgeable about educational activities. In many instances, however, reporters are either involved with a number of other activities in addition to the schools or are new enough to the job that they lack an understanding of school operations. The superintendent should provide the reporters who cover Board of Education meetings regularly with a composite file concerning the school system. It makes sense for the reporters to have available to them information concerning the school system which may be helpful in understanding the school situation and in reporting and interpreting the events to the public.

The reporters should have copies of the board policies, staff and board directories, curriculum development plans, and the calendars which establish the dates for administrative and board activities. They should have information of special activities of the school system, the plans and designs of new school buildings, bond issues, millage elections, and the like. The reporters should have as much background information as possible on all items of a particularly controversial nature. The school system's plan for desegregation, and its policy toward student activism, as well as the system's procedures for professional negotiations or collective bargaining, should be well understood by the press so that these matters can be interpreted correctly to the citizens. As a school system develops new programs and activities, it should be normal routine procedure to make copies for the press and the media.

The key word in this matter is "preparation." You cannot expect reporters to report comprehensively a complex problem without adequate background material. The time to build this background is prior to the time of the meeting when the action takes place. It would be well to insert a word of caution at this point. You need to know your reporters well enough to know whether they will accept materials in confidence or whether they feel conscious-bound to report everything they know to the public. This is a part of the understanding that the superintendent should have with the media. Some reporters are willing to discuss matters with the superintendent and keep these matters in confidence if they see a reason for it. Other reporters feel that they should alert the public to some important matter coming up before the Board of Education if it is not already generally known. The superintendent must be sure he knows which reporter reacts in which way. He should also understand that if he tells one reporter something in confidence, he may well expect opposition from other reporters who were not in on the discussion. It is certainly good procedure, whenever possible, to deal with all representatives of the media in the same fashion.

Advance Preparations for the Meeting

After the agenda has been planned and sent to the Board of Education, a copy of the agenda, plus supporting materials, should be given to representatives of the press and other media who normally cover the meetings. The superintendent should expect, and welcome, requests from the press for more detailed information on the agenda items. Whenever possible the superintendent should arrange a specific time to talk directly with the reporters who will be doing advance stories concerning the forthcoming meeting. This is particularly true for those items on the agenda which are controversial or of particular interest to certain segments of the public.

The agenda for the meeting, and all the supporting material available for publication, should be bound in a folder and indexed for the press. The reporter should have it at his fingertips as explanation for the matters to be discussed by the Board at the meeting. As was mentioned in Chapter 3, the superintendent wants to make certain that his board members receive the agenda before the press receives it. There is no reason for a board member to read in the paper about a forthcoming meeting before he has received the agenda from the superintendent. It is a rare situation when the superintendent cannot make available to the press the same information that is available to the board. The superintendent must use discretion and good judgment in making this decision. It implies a good knowledge of the working relationship by the superintendent and the reporters.

Some reporters prefer special seating arrangements in the meeting room but others prefer to be seated in the audience. Many newspaper men prefer to be cast in the role of an observer rather than in the role of a participant. However the seating arrangements are made for the press, the reporters should not appear to be a part of the official participants in the meeting. Whenever possible the seating arrangement should be left to the discretion of the reporters. If the reporters choose to have special seating arrangements, the superintendent should see to it that they are supplied with ample desk space and whatever supplies they might need. He should also see to it that the reporters who cover the meetings regularly are introduced to the individual members of the Board so they can be identified with ease by the reporter and so they will know each other.

Reporters should not interrupt the flow of the meeting to ask questions. There are rare exceptions to this, but as a general rule the reporters should be encouraged to keep a list of inquiries as the meeting progresses. A member of the superintendent's staff can be helpful in this situation if he is readily available to answer questions of the press. Many times the reporters will need to question the superintendent following the meeting concerning details that were not clear to the reporter during the meeting itself. If the superintendent feels that he will not be available to do this immediately after the meeting, a selected staff member should be available for that purpose. The public information specialist is often used in this capacity.

When meetings are to be broadcast by radio or television, the superintendent or a selected staff member should be certain that all necessary arrangements are made. Space for microphones, cameras and monitors should be planned by the superintendent, or delegated to a staff member, and not left for the technician to work out himself. Chairs and tables should be provided where necessary. Reporters for radio and television should have copies of the agenda and supporting materials in advance of the meeting. This is particularly true if they have plans to broadcast only certain portions of the meeting. The superintendent should have a selected staff member to make certain these arrangements have been made. The superintendent should have a good understanding with these reporters that they are not to disrupt the proceedings or interfere with the activities of the Board since this kind of reporting is a bit different from that of the representatives of the newspapers.

Avoiding Conflict with the Media

Every superintendent is faced with the problem of how he should react when reports of the meetings are inaccurate or misleading. Reporters are not infallible and they do make mistakes. It is also true that in some situations certain reporters will give a slant to the news as a result of their own impressions of the media. Superintendents often feel that statements made during meetings are misquoted out of context. The tape recording of the meeting can be a source for documentation if this is needed. Statements requiring precision of thought can be written for the use of the press when this is deemed advisable. The superintendent might be a bit hesitant to do this on certain occasions for fear that his comments may be too sterile or stereotyped. There are, however, several occasions on which the superintendent does not want to risk misunderstanding or improper interpretation.

There are times when the superintendent feels strongly that the reporter has reported the meeting erroneously or has slanted the coverage of the meeting, or has misquoted the superintendent or a board member, or has otherwise reported the meeting in an unsatisfactory manner. It is at this point that the superintendent can profit from the understandings and working relationships he has established in advance with the reporters and announcers. The superintendent must exercise good judgment in determining when the event is of such consequence that it needs to be brought to the attention of the reporter. If the reporter made the mistake, the superintendent should talk with the reporter first and not go directly to the editor. If the superintendent believes that the reporting is flagrantly slanted or continually erroneous, he should then feel free to carry the complaint to the reporter's immediate supervisor.

The superintendent must exercise care and judgment in pursuing this matter, and in considering the need to inform the Board of his concern and of his complaint to the reporter's supervisor. This is touchy ground for the superintendent and he is dealing with a ticklish subject when he attempts to correct poor reporting. Nevertheless, he should have that option open to him if he has done all within his power to provide the necessary information and material. The superintendent should assess the situation carefully and decide the best way to deal with the matter. If he can gain no satisfaction from talking with the reporter, he should then carry the matter to the reporter's supervisor. He should, of course, do this in an objective manner, emphasizing the fact that he is desirous of helping to correct the situation.

Many superintendents and board members have been burned badly by improper reporting of board meetings. Contrary to popular opinion, most reporters are anxious to provide fair, impartial and meaningful coverage of school activities. Very few items of concern in a community can rival the public school system for reader interest. Citizens have a great stake in their schools and will follow in detail the activities of the school system. This situation can be enhanced by newspaper, radio and television, when a proper working relationship exists between the school system and the media. When this relationship seems to be turning sour, the superintendent, as well as the media representative, should look for ways immediately to correct the situation. No one benefits when the school system and the press are at odds. An experienced superintendent said wisely once, that "you cannot afford to carry on a feud with anyone who buys ink by the barrel." By the same token, the media cannot benefit by continually harassing the schools, the superintendent, or the Board of Education. The school system should do all it can to understand the newspaper and television deadline requirements and understand that certain things must be accomplished within a certain period of time for the media to be effective. The media must understand that those in education have a primary responsibility of working in the school system and providing sound education for the children of the community. The roles are not mutually exclusive. They can be compatible if efforts are made by all concerned in that direction.

Dealing with Errors and Conflict

No school superintendent, nor school system, nor Board of Education, is right all the time. Errors of judgment are made occasionally. When these situations occur the best procedure is to admit the mistake, explain the reasons behind the decision, profit from the experience, and move on to the next matter of business. Alibiing is not a profitable occupation. A newsman will generally be more understanding and more sympathetic if a school superintendent is willing to admit on occasion that an error has been made. The above statements are also applicable to newsmen. The practical superintendent will realize, however, that he is allowed only a minimum number of these mistakes.

Representatives of media will interpret your board meetings to the public. A proper effort on the part of the superintendent can enhance the effectiveness of the reporting. Lack of concern and preparation can lead only to poor reporting and a poorly informed community. The superintendent must take time to discuss this matter carefully with his staff, and particularly with his public information officer, as well as with the Board of Education, so that all persons affected will be aware of the steps taken to ensure good relations with representatives of the various media. Members of the superintendent's staff must understand the importance the superintendent attaches to the matter of good public relations. An individual staff member, speaking at the wrong time or stating the wrong thing to a reporter, can destroy what has been a good working relationship. When staff members are involved in planning the arrangements for the media this is less likely to happen. Statements to the press concerning meetings of the Board of Education should come primarily from the superintendent or from members of the Board. Staff members should not make statements of this kind unless approved by the superintendent. This does not mean that the superintendent should issue all statements relating to the school system because other staff members can make good contributions to the public's knowledge about the school system. There should be a good understanding between the superintendent and his staff members concerning statements relating to meetings of the Board of Education.

How to Say It

One of the principal complaints school men receive from newspaper men is the use of educational jargon. A number of reporters and editors refer to this as "schooleese." They say that educators do have a jargon, more of a jargon than most other professions. They insist that school men enjoy it so much and use it so often that it is often employed at the expense of good communication. The public information specialists are quite aware of this problem, particularly if they have had any newspaper experience. Educators should be most careful to avoid this whenever possible. They should conscientiously seek the advice of the press when they are guilty of it and consider very carefully the advice the press has to offer. Those of us in education have heard this complaint for some time. Many have made real efforts to correct the situation. Some authorities have gone so far as to say that one of the major reasons for our inability to communicate with the public is our use of educational jargon and terminology. Perhaps it is worthwhile to give serious consideration to expressing our thoughts and ideas with the full intention of communicating with the public and not merely impressing them with our knowledge and vocabulary.

In spite of the best efforts that can be made to effect good relations between the school system and the media, the superintendent and the press will sometimes be at opposite poles on particular questions. Often it is a question of whether to publish or not to publish. The superintendent will feel that some matters should not be published at this time or that a particular item should be given strong publicity at this time. The press may feel quite the opposite. In this situation it is best if both respect the other's viewpoints but also respect the other's responsibility to make a decision and to act. The situation may also occur in which the press will ask for information that the superintendent feels he cannot give in good conscience. In this circumstance the superintendent should simply say that he is sorry but that his information cannot be given to them, or he can say simply, "no comment." It is better to refuse to comment or refuse to give information than it is to dodge a question by saying that you do not know the answer when you really do know. This is simply a recognition of the fact that the superintendent and the media do play different roles and that their roles do, on occasion, conflict. It is not as important to try to shape the information that the public gets as it is to do all possible to make certain that the public gets full information. If the public gets the idea that someone is trying to make them think or feel a certain way, they tend to become suspicious or resentful.

There are some sections of the country where, for some reason or other, newspapers are not interested in covering the activities of the schools. While this happens today only in isolated circumstances, it is important for the superintendent, in this kind of a situation, to develop some means for communicating with the public. He might have to consider a direct communication mailed to residents of the community which would outline the activities of the Board of Education and of the school system. He might attempt to work with newspapers in nearby communities so that the events of the school system could be covered there. In these isolated circumstances, the superintendent must make special efforts to see that the residents of the community obtain information about the operation of the local school system.

The superintendent who plans adequately for the press and other media at meetings of the Board of Education should be able to expect fair, impartial, and objective reporting. Representatives of the media should be able to expect from the superintendent the necessary information and background material. This is a two-way street, but the wise superintendent understands the necessity of taking the extra step to insure an effective working relationship.

Review of Suggested Procedures

1. Know the reporters, editors and supervisors.
2. Establish an understanding of the role of the superintendent, the Board of Education, and the representatives of the media.
3. Inform the media as completely as possible on events

to be discussed at the forthcoming meeting and provide the necessary background information.

4. Make the necessary physical arrangements for the media such as proper space, seating, lighting, etc.
5. Clarify any points of misunderstanding immediately after the meeting and before the information is presented by the media to the public.
6. Show a sincere willingness to help the reporters on any follow-up information needed, but remember that reporting the news is the role of the media, not the superintendent.

7

Evaluating the Meeting and the Planning

A s with all operations within the school system, evaluation is an important part of every school board meeting. If any program or activity is to be improved, continuing evaluation is a necessity. This particular area of board meetings is often overlooked or intentionally avoided. Some people simply fail to give thought to the need for evaluation, some are afraid to face the necessity of evaluation, and some do not involve the staff in preparations for the meeting. Whatever the reasons might be, evaluation of school board meetings is not an integral part of the program in many school systems.

If evaluation is considered to be an important part of planning and conducting school board meetings, it seems that this evaluation could take two forms. Immediate evaluation can take place as soon after the board meeting as possible. In this type of evaluation the superintendent and the planning team can recall the most recent meeting and review the meeting with an eye toward details of both the preparation and the conduct of the meeting. Long range evaluation can occur from time to time and perhaps involve others who have been involved in the meetings either as participants or as spectators. Both kinds of evaluation have validity and both are useful in enabling the Board and the superintendent to conduct effective, worthwhile meetings and to project to the community an image of efficiency and reasonableness in the total operation. This chapter considers both kinds of evaluation as they may occur by different individuals and groups.

Planning Team Evaluation

The planning team shares a good deal of the responsibility for effective board meetings under the leadership of the superintendent. Since this planning team is involved in preparation of the meeting, it follows logically that the planning team should have a major voice in evaluation of the meeting. The superintendent occupies the center stage position during the meeting itself so he is often in a difficult position to evaluate, personally, meetings of the Board of Education. Simply as a result of the position he occupies during the meeting, he must, of course, maintain an important role in the evaluation that is done by the planning team. If the evaluation that is done by the planning team is to be effective, there must exist between the planning team and the superintendent a rapport and an understanding that enables team members to react to the meeting honestly and openly. To quote a popular phrase, they should "tell it like it is." Some superintendents who are concerned about particular aspects of board meetings will appoint one or more planning team members to serve as observers in the audience during the meeting. They may be requested to watch for certain particular things during the course of the meeting, or they may serve as observers of the general tone of the meeting. Sometimes it is worthwhile for one staff member to evaluate the physical setting, the acoustics, and the general atmosphere existing during the meeting. In other situations it might be desirable for one staff member to analyze the presentations of the superintendent concerning his clarity and interpretation of facts and materials. In other instances a staff member analyzing the amount of discussion on various topics by individual board members, or by representatives of pressure groups, may be helpful in presenting the total meeting in perspective.

The planning team should meet as soon after the board meeting as possible for the evaluation of the meeting. If the board meetings are held at night, the "post-mortem" or evaluation session should be planned for the next morning. If the meetings are held during the day, it is well to arrange some time later in the day for the evaluation session. The planning team should be expected to compare the expected reactions and results with what actually occurred during the meeting. If the staff has been unable to predict either the reaction or the outcome of particular issues, with a reasonable degree of accuracy, this information can be valuable both to the superintendent and to the planning team itself. This is a good time for the team to judge the adequacy of the planning for the meeting. Was the planning sufficiently thorough so that all necessary preparations were made and that all available information was presented? Were the agenda items presented to the Board and the public in such a way that the materials could be easily understood and interpreted? Were the questions raised by board members, and others, of the type that indicated that additional information could have been helpful? What unexpected turn of events occurred during the meeting? Could these unexpected events have been prevented by better planning and preparation?

The planning team at this time would also do well to analyze the press coverage given to the meeting if sufficient time has elapsed for the media to report the meeting. Did the newspapers or other media emphasize the important activities that occurred during the meeting and did they report and interpret these matters fairly and correctly? If the superintendent and the planning team are not satisfied with the press coverage this would be a good time to reflect on the amount of information given to the press prior to the meeting, and on the whole question of dealing with the press and other media. As superintendents, we often complain about press coverage but we need to make certain that, insofar as possible, we have provided representatives of media with as much information and explanation as possible. The members of the planning team can make a valuable contribution to an evaluation of the meeting if they realize that the superintendent honestly wants and respects their opinions. If they believe, however, that the superintendent likes to hear only the good things, this is what he will generally receive from them. If the superintendent is conscientious about evaluation, he will try to establish with his planning team an atmosphere for honest evaluation with an eye toward improving the meetings of the Board of Education.

In addition to the immediate evaluation, it is well for the planning team and the superintendent to periodically evaluate the results of several meetings that have been held. As the group meets to plan the next meeting of the Board, evaluation of the past meetings can have a real impact on the preparation and planning for future needs. Many details of operation can be improved and changed to meet the particular needs of the local situation. In order to do this the planning team must be primed to look for ways to improve. This will not occur accidentally. The superintendent must work with his planning team in such a way that a spirit of constant evaluation exists as they move from one meeting to the next. In this way the planning team can become more effective in advising the superintendent concerning the efficiency and the productivity of meetings of the Board.

The Superintendent's Personal Evaluation

Since the superintendent does play a leading role in meetings of the Board, he must allow some time to view the meeting from his own perspective and analyze his personal reactions to the conduct of the meeting. He should look with a critical eye on his own presentations, his recommendations, and his participation in the meeting. Each superintendent judges for himself, in view of local situations and his own ability, the amount of involvement he should have in the meeting. No set formula exists. No one can tell you as a practicing superintendent the amount of involvement the superintendent should have in the board meeting. This is something that every superintendent must judge for himself in light of all the factors involved in his own local situation. Having decided this, in view of all of these circumstances, the evaluation of his own role in the Board of Education meetings is important if presented in the proper perspective. The purpose of this personal evaluation is to judge how well he is fulfilling the role he has envisioned for himself in the board meetings.

In addition to evaluating his own role in the meeting, the superintendent should give some thought to the general format of the agenda and to the placing of items before the Board. Were the items placed in the proper order? Would it be better in future meetings to place important items of controversy in a different place on the agenda? Was he really prepared for the opposition that came from board members on a specific proposal he made? The superintendent should give consideration to the time schedule that was planned for the meeting and compare that with the time actually spent on the material at the meeting. It is at this point that he can determine how much time he might need to give to routine items in the future.

The superintendent should give particular attention to any obvious errors he made during the meeting. Were these errors of judgment or errors in planning? Did he commit any serious errors in the matter of personal relations with either members of the Board or the public? If he could replay the particular crisis situation, would he have acted in the same manner as he did during the public meeting? This is not to say that the superintendent should spend much time in worrying about past mistakes, but he should at least recognize the errors for what they were and look for ways to avoid them in the future. The superintendent should be concerned particularly about any surprise events that occurred during the meeting. Every superintendent is going to be caught off guard occasionally, but if this situation could have been prevented by better preparation or by more thorough planning, he should make every effort to avoid a repetition of such surprises in the future.

The superintendent, in his personal evaluation, should also consider the effectiveness of the board members during the board meeting. Did any of the board members appear to need additional background information on the matter under discussion? Was antagonism present between any of the board members, or between any of the board members and the superintendent? If so, what can the superintendent do to alleviate such difficulties in the future? Public displays of antagonism and bitterness are not easy to eliminate, but the superintendent must be aware of the damage this can do to the school system and should make every effort to avoid this situation whenever possible. Sometimes it is possible to work out meetings between the involved members to resolve the conflict. Other times the services of an intermediary can be utilized. The superintendent can play this role occasionally but he should be very careful in placing himself in the middle between two warring board members. The superintendent's effectiveness in the board meeting, and in his total job performance, can be reduced considerably by finding himself in the middle of a personal conflict between two or more board members. As the superintendent evaluates this meeting he should consider very carefully what measures might be taken to eliminate public displays of animosity. But he should be very careful how he does it. The superintendent should consider also, at this time, his overall helpfulness to the board chairman in particular. If the chairman was in doubt concerning any of the issues or concerning the handling of specific matters, could the superintendent have been of assistance to the chairman without usurping the role of the chairman or without appearing to interfere in the chairman's prerogatives.

The superintendent's personal evaluation should also center on his own organization for the meeting and his presentations to the Board. If he had to delay the meeting while he searched for materials, perhaps this could be avoided in the future by better organization and planning on his part. If he did not have available certain bits of information requested by a board member, better preparation in the future might avoid this situation. It should be stated clearly at this time that there are a great number of circumstances involved in every meeting of a Board of Education that are impossible for the superintendent to predict or to plan. The superintendent must be honest with himself, however, and differentiate between those circumstances which were preventable and those which were not. If an unsatisfactory situation could have been prevented by better planning on the part of the superintendent or his team, the superintendent should benefit from this in planning future meetings. If no amount of preparation could have avoided the situation, the superintendent would do well to forget it and move on to other things. In making this personal evaluation, the superintendent would do well to write down a reminder to himself of particular things he might wish to note for succeeding meetings. They may be items to be discussed with the planning team, or they may simply be matters of a personal nature that the superintendent wants to remind himself of for future needs. The overall personal evaluation of the superintendent is extremely important in planning for meetings in the future that will be more effective and productive.

Board Evaluation

The members of the Board of Education have a great stake in the conduct of public meetings. Their opinions concerning evaluation of those meetings should be solicited by the superintendent. Each superintendent will know the best way to accomplish this in his own local situation. You must simply know your local circumstances. The superintendent must know his board members well enough to know what procedure he should adopt in working with board members in the matter of evaluation. Approaching a board member in the wrong way concerning evaluation of the meeting can do more damage than it can do good. The wise superintendent will weigh this situation very carefully before he decides what procedures he will follow in getting the opinions of his board members. Perhaps a personal conversation on other matters might lead into an evaluation of the meeting by the board member. Sometimes discussions over the telephone can be helpful. However it is done, the board members should be consulted as often as the superintendent deems desirable concerning the conduct of the meetings, the preparation for the meetings, and the amount of information supplied to the Board by the superintendent.

Board members are going to evaluate the meetings for themselves with or without the request of the superintendent, but if the board members realize the desire of the superintendent to be informed about their feelings concerning the meeting, they are more apt to be in a constructive frame of mind as they evaluate the meeting. If an atmosphere of continuing evaluation is established with board members, they will be anxious and willing to communicate their feelings to the superintendent at any time. The superintendent must, of course, be careful that he does not leave the impression that he is constantly needing assurance from the Board that all is well. He should be able to strike a balance in the minds of board members between the need for honest evaluation and opinion, and a need for reassurance or expression of confidence. Board members should not feel a necessity to constantly reassure the superintendent that all is going well. By the same token, neither should it be necessary for board members to constantly criticize the operation of the meetings. A much better route is to sit down with the superintendent, outline the complaints that exist, and attempt to reach a viable conclusion. Nothing offers better opportunity for the resolution of conflict and differences of opinion than the opportunity to sit down together and discuss the situation. At the same time, there should exist between the superintendent and the board members an understanding that allows honest and frank discussions concerning their evaluation of the meetings. Such an atmosphere of continuing evaluation cannot help but lead to improved public meetings.

Observers at the Meeting

Most school board meetings today are attended, from time to time, by various representatives of the public and by various interested individuals and groups. A number of organizations appoint members of their groups to attend school board meetings regularly. Some individuals attend out of interest and some serve as watchdogs for particular organizations. Parent-Teacher Councils, taxpayer leagues, real estate concerns, Chamber of Commerce representatives, proponents of racial integration, and other groups, are often represented at meetings of the Board. It would be appropriate for the superintendent and/or the planning team to be able to get some kind of reaction from members of the public who attend board meetings. Were they able to understand the events that transpired at the meeting? Could they follow the agenda as the Board moved from one item to the next? Do they feel that the best interests of the public are being served by the Board? Do they recognize and understand the procedures that have been established by the Board for individuals or groups wishing to present matters to the Board for consideration? Is this policy workable? Do they, as representatives of the citizenry, feel that they have an avenue by which they can approach the Board on matters of concern? The superintendent should not be reluctant to ask opinions of members of the audience at board meetings. He would, of course, not want to make this a regular practice for fear of being swayed by too many contrary opinions, but he should certainly be able to assess the general reaction of the public to meetings of the Board of Education. He should orient the members of his planning team toward the need for assessing public reaction to meetings of the Board. The superintendent should be careful in making this particular evaluation. He will understand that actions of the Board are not always pleasing to selected individuals or groups attending the meetings, but he should be able to assess through conversations with various citizens the general reaction that the public is receiving from the Board's public meetings.

Communication with the Staff

A few short years ago staff members in the school system were concerned about the results of board meetings only as these meetings affected them personally. This is no longer the case in a large number of school systems throughout the country. Staff members are assuming the position today that they have a definite interest in the activities of the Board of Education and are interested in the operations of the Board. The superintendent and his planning team should evaluate carefully the reactions of the professional staff to the board meetings. Many superintendents have become concerned over the fact that coverage of the meetings by the press does not always convey to staff members a true picture of what transpired at the meeting. As a result of this, many superintendents have instituted definite procedures for informing staff members of the precise happenings at the meetings of the Board.

Some superintendents establish meetings of their administrative and supervisory staffs immediately following the board meetings so that the actions of the Board, as well as the intent of the Board, can be related accurately to members of the staff. Other superintendents use newsletters directly to the staff as a means of communication. Some superintendents record the important events of the board meetings in publications which are mailed directly to citizens in the community. All of this is somewhat dependent upon the local situation. If press coverage is adequate it may not be necessary to devise special means of communicating with either the staff or the public. If this is not the case, however, it may be an advantage to the administrator to devise some means of direct communication with both the staff and citizenry. Regardless of the adequacy of press coverage, it is generally advantageous for the superintendent to meet with at least key members of the staff as soon after the board meeting as possible to report to the staff the significant events that occurred during the meeting of the Board. In this way direct communication can be established with these key personnel as rapidly as possible. It should be recognized that these meetings with staff members will not always produce significant events. Sometimes board meetings are conducted only for routine business. When this is the case, the report to the staff may be boring or repetitious. Over the long haul, however, it is a distinct advantage to be able to communicate with key staff members as soon as possible following meetings of the Board of Education. One of the results of evaluation of board meetings indicates that rapid and effective communication with key administrators is a distinct advantage to the operation of the school system.

It should not be too difficult to receive from staff members, both administrators and teachers, some kind of evaluation of the workings of the Board of Education. In this situation the superintendent again should use good judgment as to the procedures he establishes for this evaluation. It is not the function of the professional staff to evaluate the Board. They should not be placed in a position of evaluating publicly the activities of the Board. By the same token, it can be helpful to the superintendent if he can gain from members of the staff an impression of how staff members do evaluate the Board itself and particularly gain an insight into the image the Board projects to the professional staff. It is most desirable that the superintendent understand the general feeling that the professional staff has concerning the operation of the Board of Education. The superintendent should find this information valuable as he compiles a total evaluation of the meeting of the Board.

Because of the importance of events handled by the Board of Education, many people in the community are continually in the process of forming an image of the Board of Education. This is evaluation. It behooves the superintendent, members of the planning team, and the board members, to have some concept of how their actions are being perceived by various people in the school community. It is not sufficient to simply plan the meeting and conduct it. Constant improvement in the operation of board meetings, and in the image the Board projects to the community, can be accomplished best by a continuing process of honest evaluation. The Board and the superintendent should meet together on occasion for the express purpose of discussing the conduct of their public meetings and for analyzing the effectiveness of these meetings. It is certainly appropriate during such discussions to evaluate the role of the superintendent and the staff as well as the role of the Board of Education in these meetings. When the proper atmosphere exists, such evaluation sessions can be an important step toward improved efficiency. Where the atmosphere is not so healthy, it can at least provide a framework for study and for future evaluation and improvement. Increased productivity of meetings of the Board of Education can be achieved through honest evaluation from many sources and the implementation of those procedures that are found to be desirable as a result of evaluation.

Review of Suggested Procedures

1. Provide evaluation as an integral part of Board of Education meetings.
2. Establish a regular time for evaluation by the planning team.
3. Establish procedures for the superintendent's personal evaluation. Don't leave it to chance.
4. Get the reactions and observations of board members.
5. Examine the public reaction and coverage by the press and other media.
6. Establish at least one session per year with the Board to discuss board meetings as well as the relationship between the superintendent and the Board.
7. Provide a method for good communication with the professional staff.

8

Recording the Results
of the Meeting

Meetings of the Board of Education are reported and recorded in a number of different ways. The newspaper, radio, and television report the results of board meetings generally from the angle of those items bearing the greatest interest to the general public. Board meetings are discussed by various citizens within the community, by staff members, and on occasion by members of the student body. The only official records of Board of Education meetings are the minutes which are formally approved and adopted by the Board. Since the minutes of meetings of the Board of Education are important, and since they do constitute the only official record of the actions of the Board, it is extremely important that careful consideration be given to the minutes, to their preparation, and their adoption. There are a number of key items concerning the minutes of board meetings which the superintendent and board members should consider. It is well if the superintendent is able to discuss these questions with the Board and arrive at some agreement concerning the specifics of the preparation and distribution of the minutes. A new superintendent would do well to discuss these particular matters as early in his tenure as possible. This chapter deals with a few of the specific responsibilities involved in recording the results of the public school board meetings.

Use of Tape Recorder

The tape recorder is a valuable instrument in recording the results of the meeting. It provides a precise record of specific discussions and actions that occur at the meeting. It can be very useful as a record of the meeting and as a means of solving possible future disagreements. It also can serve as a guarantee that no one will be misquoted. Tape recordings can be very valuable in the preparation of the minutes.

Style of the Minutes

One of the first questions to be decided is the style and the format that will be used in recording the minutes of the meeting. It is appropriate to reach an understanding with the Board concerning the details of the minutes and the format to be used in preparing them. It is important, also, to discuss with the Board the volume and the length of the minutes. What is to be included? What is to be left out? It is clear that all actions of the Board that are approved or adopted by the Board must be listed and recorded in the minutes. It is generally appropriate to include the motion made as nearly verbatim as possible. This is one of the instances in which the tape recording of the meeting can be of real value. Occasionally if it is difficult to take proper notes on the motion, or if the discussion is long and complex, the actual motion may get lost in the process. The tape recording of the meeting can be valuable not only in recording the specific motion, but also in clarifying the intent of the action by the Board. It is true that some board members are not inclined to plan ahead on the motions they intend to make. Sometimes motions made are difficult to understand and are not clear and concise. Board members should be encouraged to think through their intended motions prior to the meeting if possible. This is one of the reasons why it has been suggested previously, in Chapter 3, that the background information concerning agenda items carry a written recommendation by the superintendent. When possible, the superintendent should couch this recommendation in terminology that would be applicable for a motion by a board member. Board members often find this very helpful in outlining specifically the kind of motion that needs to be made. This should not be considered an imposition on any board member because board members are free to either accept and use the recommended action, or to phrase the motion in their own words if they prefer. It is well for the superintendent to phrase his recommendation so that it can be used as a motion, however, if board members are desirous of doing so.

There is often a good deal of concern about how much discussion should be included in the minutes. Most Boards prefer to keep the minutes as brief as possible while being inclusive and comprehensive in their coverage. Occasionally there appears a need for the inclusion of discussion — general statements in the minutes. There is very rarely any need for voluminous minutes which quote verbatim the discussions and observations of various members of the Board. This does happen from time to time if board members do not trust each other or if they do not trust the superintendent, or if there is dissension between any board member and the person responsible for the preparation of the minutes. This is another reason why it is so important that the minutes be prepared accurately and precisely, and that they be prepared with complete fairness to all parties concerned. The minute a participating board member feels that the minutes have been slanted in any particular direction to either embarrass him or to fail to portray accurately his position on a particular motion, he begins to have real concern about what the minutes will show. Robert's Rules of Order can provide a guideline for the minutes if board members have difficulty deciding what ought to be included and what should be left out. A good rule of thumb, however, is to include in the minutes only those actions that were adopted by the Board, and any directions given by the Board to the superintendent in relation to interpretation of policies or specific problem areas within the school system. The minutes should be as brief as possible to cover the subjects completely.

Who Does the Job?

Procedures for assigning responsibilities for taking minutes vary considerably from one place to another. Some communities have elected board secretaries. In many cases the superintendent is responsible for the minutes. He often delegates this responsibility to a secretary or other staff member. Occasionally a board member is charged with the responsibility of keeping minutes. If the superintendent is the one responsible for the minutes, how is this best accomplished? Any superintendent who has spent at least one week on the job knows that a competent secertary is worth her weight in gold. This is particularly true in the preparation and distribution of the minutes of the board meeting, and in serving as a secertary and note-taker at meetings of the Board. Once the responsibility for taking minutes is assigned to a staff member or secretary, every provision should be made to clarify the responsibility as completely as possible. The secretary should have a good knowledge of short-hand and the other basic secretarial skills. She should certainly record every motion that is made and the person seconding the motion. This is important because following a lengthy discussion, the chairman will frequently ask for the motion to be repeated. It is important that the secretary be able to repeat the motion accurately and carefully.

Following the meeting a rough draft of the minutes of the meeting should be compiled as soon as possible. You shouldn't allow your memory to get clouded or your notes to get cold. Regardless of who is responsible for taking the minutes and for the initial preparation of the minutes, the superintendent still bears the final responsibility for the minutes as they are distributed to the Board. Consequently he should review the rough draft of the minutes very carefully to make certain that all necessary items have been included and that they have been phrased in a way that will be satisfactory, concise, and fair. Once the rough draft is completed the final copies are prepared and mailed as directed.

Taking and Recording the Minutes

There are a few important details to remember that are involved in taking, transcribing, and recording the minutes of school board meetings. It is important to locate the secretary in a position where she can both see and hear the board members and the superintendent. If she has difficulty hearing the discussion, she will have difficulty in recording accurately the activities of the Board. She must definitely be aware of the background material that has been presented to the Board as part of the agenda preparation. If the superintendent is responsible for the minutes, and if he uses the same secretary for recording the minutes as he does for preparation of agenda items, then there is no problem concerning the secretary being informed and knowledgeable about the agenda. If for any reason different personnel are involved in the preparation of agenda items and materials, and for the taking of minutes at the meetings, it is extremely important that the secretary responsible for the minutes be given a copy of the background material and advised concerning various items appearing before the Board. It is recommended, whenever possible, that the person responsible for taking minutes and preparing them for approval be acquainted with the activities of the school system, the immediate problems under consideration, and the administrative response to the problem. It is extremely difficult for a person without this background information to have a good understanding of the discussion and the action of the Board. She simply needs to be knowledgeable about school events in order to understand fully the situation being discussed. Simple errors through a lack of background information or an erroneous interpretation can become very serious if not corrected.

It is important in preparing a draft of minutes to be able to sift through the events occurring at the meeting and identify those to be included in the minutes. This is a place where experience in the local situation is invaluable. The secretary taking the minutes must also have information available on items requiring great detail. This is particularly true in such topics as bid compilations, lengthy quotations, board resolutions, property descriptions, and items of this nature. Both the superintendent and the secretary should be aware constantly that minutes of the Board are official records. As such they are open to audit and are referred to constantly as the primary source of information and reference concerning past actions of the Board of Education.

Promptness in the distribution of minutes to board members depends on a great number of factors. The amount of help available, schedule, local customs, time available, and other factors enter into the promptness with which minutes can be handled. Some school systems must assign a person full time to provide and care for minutes. In some smaller operations, the superintendent himself assumes the responsibility for this. This is not good practice and is certainly not recommended. The superintendent has enough to do during the meeting without trying to remember and record all of the specifics of board action. The superintendent and board members should agree in essence on a flexible time schedule for the distribution of minutes to the board members. It should be recognized that promptness is an important factor. It should be recognized, also, that the available staff and available time are also to be considered. It is important to note, at this time, that the minutes do not become official minutes of the board meeting until they have been formally adopted at a subsequent meeting of the Board. They are not official when they are circulated to board members for review. Once they are adopted, however, they do become the official record for the school system.

Indexing of Minutes

Since minutes of the meetings of the Board of Education are official records, every school system is charged with the responsibility of maintaining these records over a period of years. The more voluminous the records become, the more difficult it is to locate past actions of the Board on specific subjects. It is important, therefore, that the school system devise some plan for indexing the minutes of the school board meetings. Generally the minutes are filed in a minute book which is bound and placed in a convenient location. A definite pattern of indexing the minutes should be established. They would, of course, be indexed chronologically by the dates of the meetings. In addition, it is very useful to have the minutes indexed by subject area and cross indexed by subject, by school, by area of interests, or in any other way that might be appropriate for that particular school system. The cross indexing of minutes can be either an elaborate system or a relatively simple one. It depends a great deal upon the needs of the school system. The superintendent, or the person responsible for the minutes, is called on quite frequently to consult the minutes of previous meetings for references on particular board actions. If there is no adequate cross indexing system, it becomes very difficult and very time consuming to locate the necessary information. The superintendent would do well to determine what the school system's needs are in relation to locating past board actions, then to establish a system for indexing the minutes of board meetings. If it appears that going back over a number of years would be an insurmountable task, it might be appropriate to begin an indexing system as of a certain year. Due to the increasing complexity of school systems, it will be more important all the time for school systems to have the capability of locating quickly past actions of the Board of Education. It is to the school system's advantage to devise some system for locating easily the minutes of those previous meetings. Some systems are using microfim, and other procedures of miniaturization, in order to conserve space. Cross indexing in these situations is even more important. The superintendent, and the school system in general, will find that indexing and cross indexing of minutes of the Board of Education meetings will be worth the effort.

Many school boards today also maintain a supplementary minute file. This is used for the filing and recording of particularly voluminous materials which may be referred to in the official minute books but are too cumbersome to include therein. In states where it is required to maintain complete files on bid tabulations, personnel approvals, and bid waivers, a supplementary minute file can be of great value. Lengthy agreements or plans, specific contracts that need to be recorded, and other such matters, can be filed in the supplementary minute file and referred to in the regular minutes. For example, it may be noted in the minutes that the Board approved the bid of a certain company on science equipment for the school system. The successful bidder and the amount of the bid can be included in the regular minute book and a reference made at that time indicating that the total bid tabulation listing all the bids received, an analysis of the bids, the report of the evaluation committee, and an explanation of any bids rejected, will be found in the supplemental minute file. This can be a real advantage to many school systems where such records are necessary.

Distribution of Minutes

One of the items that should be decided by the Board of Education and the superintendent pertains to the distribution of the minutes. A decision should be made regarding the number of people or organizations that should receive copies of the minutes after they have been approved by the Board. It is generally con-

sidered appropriate that only the board members receive copies of
the minutes prior to the time they are approved at the subsequent
meeting. Once these minutes have been approved and adopted
officially, however, the superintendent should have a definite list of
individuals or groups to whom minutes will be mailed. The question
might be asked, why is this important? It is important in order to
avoid disputes and problems that often arise today concerning
official actions of the Board.

Some Boards distribute minutes to a large number of individuals and groups within the community. In other situations no one
receives a copy of the official minutes after they have been adopted.
Situations vary greatly from one community to the next. More and
more organizations today are interested in actions of the Board
of Education. More and more organizations are acting as lobbyists or
pressure groups to the Board. The local education association, the
local union, the PTA Council, the Chamber of Commerce, the
taxpayer league, the retired citizens associations, and a great variety
of other organizations often want to be included on the list to
receive copies of both the agendas and the official minutes. If the
Board has no set policy on the distribution of official minutes, it
is often left to the discretion of the superintendent to decide whether
or not he should accede to a request of a particular group for a
copy of the minutes. When he complies with one request, it is
then difficult for him to refuse the request of another organization,
even if that organization is notoriously unfriendly to the school
system or is at the present time in concentrated opposition to the
school system on a particular matter.

If the official minutes of the Board can be given to organizations which request them, then should they not also be given to
any individual who requests them? It is true, unfortunately today,
that every community has some isolated individuals who take it
upon themselves to attempt to influence the activities of the Board
of Education in many devious means. Every practicing superintendent is acquainted with some individuals answering that descrip-
tion. They demand to be a part of the on-going activities of the
Board of Education or of the school system. They often want
special attention and special recognition. They can cause the super-

intendent, or other school officials and board members, considerable consternation and a great deal of time and effort in many facets of the school operation. They quite often desire and insist upon minutes of the board meetings. Every school Board is in a better position if a decision can be made concerning the distribution of the official minutes prior to the time that any difficulty arises over the minutes. This is not to deny the fact that minutes of the Board of Education meetings are public records. They should be made available to the public. This availability, however, should be according to a set procedure established by the Board which is consistent with state law, regulation and custom. As with many other matters in school administration, it is better to build the bridge before you need it than to find yourself sadly immersed in water over your head and struggling to stay afloat. The Board would do well to adopt a specific procedure concerning the distribution of minutes before it becomes a major issue raised by some interested party.

The Need for Care

It should be emphasized once again that the minutes of the meetings of the Board of Education are official records. They are referred to constantly. In essence, the minutes represent the last word as far as actions of the Board are concerned. How today's minutes are recorded may not seem too important at the moment, but a lack of concern for specifics or for proper interpretation may come back to haunt you at some time in the immediate future. Some examples of this particular situation may be found in almost every school system in this country. A resolution adopted by the Board two years ago may turn out to be extremely important in resolving an issue arising this month. Property deeds and titles should be accurately defined. Occasionally the action of a Board on a particular bid or quotation or purchase may be challenged. Reference will be made immediately to the minutes of that meeting to determine whether the action of the Board was in conformance with the prescribed statutes or regulations. The recording of salary schedules is extremely important in those states where it is required. A number of school systems have found to their utter dismay that a small error in recording salary schedules became very costly at a later date. Particular attention should be given to the recording of contracts and tenure status for teachers. Almost every case involving the dismissal of a tenure teacher will result in a careful scrutiny of the minutes which reflect the actions of the Board. In many states the validity of the action may rest primarily on whether or not the Board followed the established legal procedures. If this is not indicated in the minutes, the Board sometimes experiences great difficulty in proving its case. The appointment, transfer, and dismissal of personnel must be effected in many states by action of the Board. Inaccuracy in these situations can lead to real difficulty for the Board. In most states only the Board of Education has the right to expell students from school, while individual school principals have the authority to suspend students for a limited period of time. Student expulsion is a very serious matter and the need for a careful recording of this action cannot be overemphasized. In all cases where the Board must be concerned about state law or State Board of Education Regulations, extreme care should be taken with the minutes so that the minutes reflect that the proper procedures were followed by the Board.

School systems today find themselves involved in court cases with greater regularity than ever before. The official minutes of the board meetings are often used in such situations. It is generally too late at this time to add any interpretation to the minutes. The records stand for themselves. The school attorney should be helpful in reviewing minutes. He can look at the minutes with an eye toward legal requirements and legal implications that might avoid serious problems in the future. The superintendent might find it worth his time to submit regularly a copy of the minutes to the attorney for review prior to adoption by the Board. This procedure would assure the superintendent and the Board a little more protection against future problems.

In summary, it can be said that the importance of accurate minutes is often overlooked. You don't do a lot with the minutes but what you do is extremely important. It behooves every superintendent and board member to give close attention to the preparation, adoption, distribution, and filing of the minutes of meetings of the Board of Education.

Review of Suggested Procedures

1. The Board and the superintendent should determine the style and format for the minutes.
2. The superintendent should always screen and approve drafts of the minutes prior to writing them in final form.
3. Set a reasonable time table for mailing minutes to board members and make plans to abide by it.
4. Minutes should be carefully bound, properly stored, and efficiently indexed and cross indexed.
5. Determine the pattern of distribution of minutes after approval by the Board.
6. Minutes are official records and will be referred to for years to come. Be accurate in their preparation.

9

Initiating Effective Follow-Up Procedures

A ctions occur at every meeting of the Board of Education which require some kind of follow-up activity on the part of the superintendent and his staff. The efficiency with which the superintendent conducts the business of the school system reflects on the image the community has not only of the superintendent but also of the total school system. If meetings of the Board of Education are to be productive affairs, action must follow the meetings. It is at this point that the total amount of planning and preparation becomes meaningful as discussion and decisions are converted into plans for action and progress. This chapter deals with procedures for initiating action as an outgrowth of meetings of the Board of Education.

Responsibility of the Superintendent

The superintendent is the executive officer of the Board of Education and is charged with the administration of the school system by the Board. He is selected by the Board for this purpose. When the Board makes a decision on a particular matter it becomes the responsibility of the superintendent to carry out that decision. He generally has the authority to implement the decision within the guidelines established by the Board's policy and to assign staff members specific responsibilities for implementation.

In the excitement of a controversial board meeting, or in the dullness and apathy of a quite routine meeting, it is possible for the superintendent to overlook some area of concern to which he should attend. It is good procedure for the superintendent to assign someone on his staff with the responsibility of listing all those activities which require action following the meeting. This is particularly true if the meeting is complex and involves a variety of different subject areas. In this kind of a situation the superintendent should not leave the matter to chance, nor should he trust his memory exclusively. The staff member or secretary assigned this responsibility should make notes of these items as they occur during the meeting, then compile these for the superintendent and make this available to the superintendent immediately following the meeting. The superintendent may wish to have this list broken down into those areas which require immediate attention, and those which can be spread over a period of time. It should be remembered, however, that those items which can be put off until a later time are the easiest ones to forget to complete. The more difficult and more controversial the matter is, or the touchier it is in terms of administrative responsibility, the easier it is to put it off.

In studying this list of required follow-up activities, it is good practice for the superintendent to establish a timetable for initiating these follow-up procedures. This timetable would include desirable dates for beginning the study or implementation as required and the dates for completion of the project for early submission to the Board or reporting to the Board. This will depend somewhat on the urgency of the matter, the scope of the problem, and the amount of staff available to handle the situation. Having perused the list and established priorities for action, the superintendent should then meet with his planning team to implement the actions of the Board.

Work with the Planning Team

The superintendent should discuss with the planning team the actions that need to be taken as a result of the board meeting. At this time they should identify the board action and discuss ways and means of implementing that action. The assignment of responsibilities to various staff members could be made at this time and target dates can be established. This is the stage, on any project that will require a considerable period of time to finish, to establish progress report periods so that the superintendent will be informed concerning the progress being made. The superintendent should also check carefully on the accountability for each of the staff members to be involved in the project. There should be no doubt in anyone's mind concerning the person to whom he reports directly about his progress on the project. The superintendent might do well at this time to note on his calendar the dates when certain progress reports are due or when projects are to be completed. This is another item he should not leave to chance or to his memory.

Inform the Staff

Once the project has been planned and organized by the planning team, and other participants in the project, the staff involved should be informed of the board action and of the procedures that have been designed to implement the necessary follow-up activities. It is important at this time to explain the reasons behind the decision, to provide some background information on the matter, and to verify the importance of the activity. It is also appropriate to discuss with the staff the difficulties that might be faced in the project as well as the possibilities that exist for progress and improvement. The superintendent should establish with the staff the required target dates for completion of the project. He should explain to them why these dates have been established and leave little doubt that he anticipates that the project will be completed by that time. The superintendent should also inform the staff of the effect this project might have on the total school system, on specific schools, or on individuals and groups within the school system. He should also take note with the staff of any effect this might have on the total community and what the reaction of the total community might possibly be. In short, the superintendent should inform the staff as completely as possible as to the actions of the Board and the follow-up procedures that have been designed for implementation of the Board's decisions.

Report to the Board

The superintendent should make provisions for reporting to the Board his action for initiating follow-up procedures as a result of actions taken at the last meeting of the Board. This can be a part of the superintendent's regular communication with the Board, or if circumstances warrant, it can be in the form of a special report to the Board. He should list the board action, and describe for the Board the follow-up procedures that have been established. He should list the target dates and the time patterns that have been established, as well as the delegation of responsibilities to various staff members. The importance of the issue and its complexity will determine how specific the superintendent might want to be in this report to the Board.

In reporting to the Board the superintendent may wish to stress the amount of staff and community involvement in the project or the activity. He would want to stress where the responsibility for successful completion of the project has been placed and indicate to the Board an approximate time when the matter can either be consummated or a progress report made to the Board. He should stress whatever administrative considerations are involved, and should certainly report all financial implications. This is particularly true when the Board adopts additional programs which are reimbursed and sponsored by the federal government. Many board members today simply do not understand the complexities of operation of federal educational programs. Neither do they appreciate the financial considerations of dealing with programs of this type. It is important, particularly in federal programs, that the superintendent explain to the Board both the effective date of the program and the funding level as well as the period of authorization. So many times it is difficult to explain why a federal program can be approved and the money still not authorized until a later date. The superintendent should also indicate to the Board in this report whether or not a full report will be made to the Board and approximately when the Board can expect such a report if it is to be made.

The purpose of the past two sections has been to emphasize the need for the superintendent to work continuously at maintaining effective lines of communication with the staff and the Board concerning actions of the Board of Education.

While these procedures suggested above may not suit your particular school system, the important thing is to guarantee that some means of implementing effective follow-up procedures is established in your school system. It is very embarrassing for a superintendent to be questioned by a board member, or a citizen, or member of the press, concerning his action on an item that was adopted by the Board at a previous meeting, and the superintendent often finds that he must quickly think of some excuse why he has not implemented the action of the Board. The fast thinking superintendent, who is quick on the draw, may be able to offer a satisfactory explanation now and then, but any consistently evasive attitude leads to suspicion and concern on the part of all those involved. All of this can be avoided if the superintendent establishes an organized, effective procedure for following up the activities of the Board of Education meetings.

Begin Planning the Next Meeting

If the superintendent has not already started his file for the next meeting of the Board of Education, he should do so immediately following the most recent meeting. He should have available in his desk a folder where items for the next meeting can be placed. This is another one of the ways in which his secretary can play a very valuable role in preparing for future meetings of the Board. The planning team at this stage should also point toward the next board meeting and begin to consider those items which the Board must study at the next meeting. This is the time to consider and discuss those long range plans that were mentioned in Chapter 3. Along with planning for the next meeting, the planning team should also consider its evaluation of the last meeting and the relation of that evaluation to subsequent meetings. This evaluation was discussed in some detail in Chapter 7. It is at this time that the planning team and the superintendent can establish due dates for materials to be in and dates for the preparation and compilation of materials and the mailing of agendas to board members. It is also the appropriate time to check on any loose strings that might be dangling from the last meeting. It begins to be clear early in the professional life of a school superintendent that the planning, conducting, evaluating, follow-up of board meetings, and planning for subsequent meetings is a continuous cycle of involvement and participation. The sooner the superintendent establishes a working pattern for this operation, the better the organization will become and the better chance for productive, efficient board meetings and effective administration.

Administrative Efficiency

The more complex a school system and the job of the superintendent, the more difficult it is to implement precisely the actions of the Board of Education. The more pressed the superintendent is with a myriad of controversial matters and difficult decisions, the more necessary it becomes for him to be well organized in all of his administrative responsibilities. The more arduous his task, and the more demanding his position becomes, the more it becomes clear that delegation of responsibility is a necessity. Few superintendents today can operate as individuals and no superintendent can do all of the administrative tasks which are necessary for the successful operation of the school system or the successful implementation of the decisions of the Board of Education.

One simple example can illustrate the necessity for delegation of responsibility and effecting follow-up procedures for the board action. We can assume that for some time the Board of Education of our school district has been interested in the program of tax sheltered annuities for members of the professional staff. For the past few years all of the business on tax sheltered annuities has been placed with one company that presented the only good plan available. In recent months the local life underwriters association has filed a petition with the superintendent and has requested the Board to study the situation so that more companies might be involved in the tax sheltered annuity business. We can assume, further, that the Board heard the petition of the underwriters association and requested the superintendent to study the matter and report to the Board with his recommendation. What follow-up procedures would you use in such a situation? Your pattern of action will be dictated somewhat by the complexity of the system and by a hundred other details, but some kind of organization is necessary in order to get the job done which the Board desires. It would seem logical for the superintendent to have on his list of follow-up activities the necessity of reporting to the Board at some future date concerning the tax sheltered annuity program. In his meeting with the planning team he would discuss with them the best way to proceed. This would certainly involve the assignment of responsibilities and the delegation of authority for the study. The superintendent, with the advice of the planning team, might well make the following assignments:

1. The assistant superintendent for business will contact the insurance consultant employed by the Board for advice on the establishment of guide lines for participation of other companies. He could gain from the consultant an opinion on how we might best obtain information from the various companies in such a form that the information could be easily compared and evaluated. He could discuss with the consultant the feasibility of a questionnaire to be distributed to the interested companies so that the necessary technical information concerning the plan and its benefits and obligations could be understood. He should also determine any recommendation he might make concerning the limitation that should be placed on the number of companies that might be permitted to participate if a limit seems to be desirable.

2. The administrative assistant might request the local education association or the union to appoint a committee to assist in the study. This committee might consider a poll of the staff representatives for ideas and opinions concerning the amount of interest in tax sheltered annuities, the types of annuities desired, the kinds of benefits that might seem desirable, withdrawal clauses and qualifying conditions. He might further investigate the possibility of using a working committee for any intensive study with the staff that might be necessary.

3. The director of finance might meet with a committee from the life underwriters association to get their suggestions and opinions and see what technical advice might be available from them. He would, of course, not obligate the school system in any way at this point but

simply discuss with them our proposed procedures and gain from them their opinion of the procedure and any suggestions they might have to assist in the study. The role of the insurance consultant should be spelled out to the life underwriters association so that it is understood that professional advice and assistance is available to the school administration.

4. The coordinator of data processing would check the capability of the school system's accounting machines and ascertain the number of deductions now being made and what capability exists for future deductions. He should also determine how many different companies might be handled conveniently by the deduction system. In addition he should ascertain the amount of reporting that might be necessary if a number of companies were involved in the program.

The assignment of these and other responsibilities would be coupled with an establishment of the next steps in the study after the data and the reports are in. It would be well to consider other items that might be affected by this change. Target dates should be established. It should also be made clear to whom each of these individuals is responsible for reporting the results of his activities. This procedure should be outlined to the staff so that they understand what progress is being made concerning tax sheltered annuities. The superintendent should then inform the Board concerning the steps that were taken, the procedures that are going to be followed, the target dates that have been set, and when the Board might reasonably expect to receive progress reports from the superintendent. If the superintendent is able to clarify a date when a recommendation might be forthcoming, he should indicate this also.

The above procedure, or some variation of it, is probably followed at the present time by most all school superintendents. It is true that this kind of matter, which is considered by the Board, the staff, and at least parts of the community to be quite important, almost demands an organized follow-up procedure. The trouble is that there are many other matters which appear to be minor or routine that are often overlooked. Even with the best preparation the superintendent may occasionally forget to initiate a follow-up procedure on some specific action of the Board, but this should not happen very often, and it should not happen at all if the superintendent can possibly avoid it. It is worthwhile to remember that the Board of Education represents the citizens of the community. The board works with the school system directly through the superintendent of schools. If the superintendent is effective and efficient in his work with the Board of Education, the Board will generally assume that the school system is effectively managed and operated, and they will generally be right.

Review of Suggested Procedures

1. Assign a staff member or secretary the responsibility of listing for you all matters requiring follow-up action.
2. Consult with the planning team and assign responsibilities for implementation.
3. Set target dates and deadlines.
4. Inform the staff and the Board of the procedures to be followed.
5. Begin planning for the next meeting.

10

The Board
and the Superintendent
Work Together

It is almost a foregone conclusion that in order for meetings of the Board of Education to be productive and efficient, the Board and the superintendent must work together. They must establish an understanding of the procedures they will follow and how those procedures can be used to increase their effectiveness. Both the Board and the superintendent must understand the importance of their activities and how each contributes to the successful operation of the school system. The Board and the superintendent cannot work against each other for any period of time without the results being damaging to the entire school system. As the Board and the superintendent develop means for working together effectively, the entire productivity of the operation is increased. This chapter deals with recognizing the powers of the Board, establishing a commitment to education, and defining as precisely as possible the roles played by the Board and the superintendent in the specific operations of the school system.

Understanding the Powers of the Board

The Board of Education sets the tone for education in the community. Progress in education in the local area is reflected primarily through actions of the Board. In most states the powers of the Board of Education can be classified into at least two categories. Those powers which are legal powers are granted by state statutes and by State Board of Education Regulations. Implied powers are those which are given to the Board in a general sense as necessary for the successful operation of the school system. Board members should have a definite understanding of both their legal and implied powers.

It is a responsibility of the board members to become informed concerning the powers of the Board. The superintendent has a responsibility in the orientation of new board members to make certain that they understand the legal and implied powers of the Board, as well as the limitations on the authority of individual board members, and on the Board acting as a legal representative of the people. The State School Board's Association and the National School Board's Association are both helpful in defining the powers of the local Board of Education. The superintendent will do well to use the services of these organizations in orienting his new board members in this direction. A good understanding on the part of the board members and the superintendent, of the powers and limitations of the Board, is necessary as early in the tenure of board members as possible.

State statutes vary considerably concerning powers and limitations of the local Board of Education. What may be an obligation of the Board in one state can be reserved for the state Board of Education in a different area of the country. What may be a task of the superintendent in one state may be a statutory obligation of the Board in another state. It is a duty of the superintendent to assist the board members in developing a precise understanding of the powers and duties of the Board of Education in his state. He can also convey to the board members those local customs and traditions which influence the powers of the local Board. In short, the powers of the Board of Education must be completely understood by the board members and the superintendent if they are to perform their tasks effectively.

Establishing a Commitment to Education

Many board members are often confused concerning what the community wants from education. It is an unfortunate fact that many Boards of Education do not know what the people of the community really want for education. Many school systems today move ahead with programs and services without a public understanding of those programs. Many Boards of Education feel that the community realizes the importance of certain school activities, and are committed to them, only to find out too late that the community was not at all interested in the particular program being developed. They discover, sometimes, that the community has real opposition to the course of action determined by the Board of Education. In fact, many school systems today are finding it increasingly difficult to pass local bond issues and millage elections. There are, of course, many reasons for this. In some cases it is simply a reflection of community opposition to any increase in the local tax roll. In some cases the community is exhibiting a reaction against the high cost of operation of all public programs. Yet in many communities, the people stand in opposition to certain programs due to a lack of established commitment to education. What does the community want? At what level should education be supported in the community? Does the community have an established commitment to education? These are questions that the Board and the superintendent must consider together. It is important to note that such decisions are not made overnight, nor for that matter, over a short period of time. They are generally made over an extended period of time and often involve a number of different school Boards and school superintendents. It is time well spent, however, if the Board and the superintendent together study the matter of local commitment to education and determine whether this commitment needs to be strengthened, defined more accurately, or whether in effect it has ever been identified at all. The Board can sometimes get a good picture of the feeling of the community through the use of such techniques as advisory committees, questionnaires to the public, and through the Parent Teacher Associations.

How is a commitment to education generally made? Often it comes as a result of tradition. It seems fair to state that school systems often find themselves in a certain orbit within the state. One can usually identify school systems which have quality education programs as those which spend a great amount of money per pupil. While this is not always an indication of quality, it is at least one measure that can be determined objectively. It can be observed that when a school system is established within a certain orbit or pattern, it moves out of that pattern only rarely and then only as a result of certain stimuli.

It is generally true that when the state legislature votes a substantial increase in state funds to local schools, this does not cause a significant change in the orbit in which the school operates. Even a decided increase in local financial effort within a particular year does not often change the general standing of the school system in relation to other school systems in the state. This is true because of the competitive nature of school systems and their desire to remain at a level nearly commensurate with the level of operation of its neighbor. It is difficult for a school system to change positions. It is difficult for the school system to move ahead of other school systems in the state to any substantial degree in a short period of time unless a definite, pronounced, established commitment is made by the local community. This happens in only two or three ways.

Sometimes leadership exercised by a new superintendent is responsible for a change in direction of the school system. This seems to be particularly true only if the community is willing to accept a new commitment, or a new sense of direction. A new superintendent is expected to produce certain changes in the school system. The important question involves whether these changes constitute any change in the commitment of the local community to education. A superintendent new to the community is in the best position to institute change in the school system. He is in the best position to increase and strengthen the commitment of the community to education. He is recognized by most observers of education as the chief change agent within the school system. If the community is to strengthen its commitment to education, the superintendent, either new or experienced, is in the best position to accomplish this.

New leadership on the Board of Education is another means of effecting a change in the commitment of the local community to education. This board leadership can be either in the form of individuals who provide real leadership for the school system, or in the form of a newly elected majority of the Board. This change in board membership often reflects a change in the attitude of the citizens of the community. Sometimes the citizenry desires a greater commitment to education and sometimes it desires a lesser commitment. Sometimes the election of new board members reflects dissatisfaction with the current operation of the school system and a desire for more progress in the schools. Both the board members and the superintendent should attempt to analyze what the selection of new board members really means in terms of community commitment to education. It is true, frequently, that an individual board member, with a personal dedication to education, can provide a real incentive for improved commitment to education. Such a board member with true leadership potential can lead the rest of the Board and the community toward improvements in the educational program and toward a greater understanding of the need for progress in education. It is likewise true that several new board members can exercise greater influence in the involvement of the community in educational change and accomplishment. Some board members newly elected to the position are reluctant to press for change in the local operation for fear of being branded as radicals, or as uncooperative individuals. There is, of course, a point to be made concerning the need for new board members to understand fully the local situation before requesting drastic changes, but new leadership on the Board is one effective means of producing a change in the commitment of the community to the educational program.

An increased amount of community involvement and understanding is another means of producing a change in the commitment of the community to education. Many local Boards of Education have discovered that comprehensive programs designed to involve the community more completely in the educational operations have resulted in a greater commitment to educational progress. Citizens are often opposed to educational change when they are unaware of the need for the change, or when they are only partially informed. No school system can expect significant improvement in the level of education offered in the local community without a comprehensive program of public information and involvement. The Board and the superintendent, working together, can produce an effective change in the level of commitment of the community if the citizens are informed completely about the operations of the school system, and if they can see the established need for change.

Another means of up-grading the educational commitment to the community is through a program aimed specifically in that direction. This has been accomplished in a few isolated school systems by simply challenging citizens of the local community to establish a level of education which is considerably higher than that previously enjoyed. This does not happen very often but it is possible. It is more likely that the commitment to education of the local community will develop gradually over a period of many years and will be changed only by specific actions of the Board and superintendent working together. Attacking this problem of educational commitment should be a priority of Boards of Education. A school system will not make significant advances without this commitment. The commitment to better education will not be made by the public without good leadership on the part of the Board and the superintendent together. The Board and the superintendent should both understand that isolated, fragmented progress can be made periodically without a total community commitment, but that substantial, regular progress will not be made without such commitment. Somehow or other the Board and the superintendent must analyze the commitment to education that currently exists in the community and search for the means to enhance that commitment. This requires, first of all, a commitment on the part of the board members and the superintendent. If the Board and the superintendent are not satisfied with the orbit in which the system now operates, they must search for those means by which to propel the school system out of one orbit into a more desirable one. This will generally require much better communications with the public and a greater sense of involvement of the public in the local school system operation. If the Board and the superintendent can secure a greater commitment to education by the local community, they will have taken the first step toward improved educational opportunity for the students of that school system.

As the Board makes decisions from one meeting to the next, it establishes a pattern for commitment to education of that community. Today the challenge is greater than at any time in our past. There is more struggle for the local tax dollar and more demands for the time and the influence required for successful school operations. Real progress by the Board on behalf of the school system can be accomplished through public meetings of the Board providing that both the Board and the community adopt a commitment to education which is harmonious and on which there is general agreement. The Board cannot get too far ahead of the community nor should it lag behind the expectations of the community. One of the superintendent's primary tasks is to assist the Board in understanding the expectations of the community and in leading the Board toward the establishment of a sound commitment to education.

The Role of the Board and the Superintendent

If the Board of Education and the superintendent are to work together cooperatively, they must establish and understand the role that each plays in the operation of the local school system. A clear understanding is essential for the successful operation of the schools. There must be established a sound basis for the definition of the functions of the superintendent and the functions of the Board of Education.

Certain basic assumptions can be made to help clarify the roles and responsibilities of the Board of Education and the superintendent. Some of these assumptions are:

1. Public education is the responsibility of the state. Under the state's constitution and legislative acts the structure has been established for the operation and control of the public schools in the local community.
2. A large measure of the responsibility for the public schools is vested in local school districts established under the laws of the state.
3. The local school Board is the agency designated by the state to represent the people of the local district and the state. The Board is charged with the responsibility to interpret the educational needs and desires of the people and to translate them into policies and program.
4. School administrators, teachers, and all other members of the school district are employed because certain services, functions, and unique skills and abilities are needed in the fulfillment of the tasks of the school district.
5. The superintendent of schools is employed by the Board

of Education as its executive agent. He is the professional advisor to the Board, the chief administrator of the schools, the leader of the staff, and the focal point of responsibility within the school system.

Practically all articles written about superintendent-Board relationships make it clear that the Board of Education is responsible for administering the policies established by the Board. The difficulty lies in defining more precisely the functions of policy-making as opposed to the functions of administration.

Recent studies have documented the fact that lack of understanding of the responsibilities and the boundaries of their jobs is a prime source of administrator-Board trouble. What makes this extremely important for all the people is that administrator-Board troubles inevitably damage the system all the way into the classrooms. If you could only use one measure in the appraisal of a school system, a good method would be to take a reading of the Board-superintendent relationships. A school district can have all the other advantages available and yet the schools would be in jeopardy if the Board and administrator were failing in their responsibilities to each other.

Many aspects contribute to the achievement of cooperation and school leadership within a school system, but the key is with the school Board and the superintendent. The real problem is to determine as completely as possible that an understanding exists between the superintendent and the Board of Education as to the roles and functions of each. It must be understood further that not all possibilities of conflict can be discussed in advance. An atmosphere of understanding must be constructed in order to solve those problems arising out of "gray" areas where it is difficult to determine specifically the functions of the Board as related to the functions of the superintendent.

While it is impossible to cover every area of school operation, the following chart endeavors to outline the functions of the superintendent and the Board of Education in various specific areas of mutual concern. The chart is not meant to be complete. It can be used as an example for further delineation of functions of the superintendent and the Board. Is is understood that this procedure may vary from one school system to another due to state laws and regulations, local custom and expediency, but the general format can be helpful in defining the roles to be followed.

GENERAL FUNCTIONS

Board of Education

Establishes general policy and rules and regulations regarding:

    employment of superintendent

    employee personnel functions

    instructional program

    pupil personnel functions

    school plant functions

    public relations functions

Superintendent

Assumes charge of school system as the executive officer of the Board of Education.

Coordinates the work of all schools and departments.

Recommends policies to the board, providing data which will permit the Board to formulate policy.

Executes policies of Board and supervises the work of those who are responsible for the administrative activities of individual schools or departments.

Reports to the Board relative to the execution of its policies and the general administration of the schools.

PERSONNEL FUNCTIONS

Board of Education

Adopts salary schedules for all personnel.

Determines the number of teachers and other employees in the school system after considering the recommendations of the superintendent.

Determines all policies relating

Superintendent

Appoints, promotes, transfers, retires, and removes all employees in the school system, and takes any other established personnel action consistent with state law and board policy.

Supervises the work of all employees of the school district.

Board of Education

to personnel including sick leave, leaves of absence, and special benefits.

Determines the policies of general personnel management.

Superintendent

Recommends all personnel policies for board action.

Executes all personnel policies adopted by the Board.

INSTRUCTIONAL PROGRAM FUNCTIONS

Board of Education

Determines the general scope of the instructional program in accordance with state laws and regulations.

Discusses and evaluates reports presented to it by the professional staff members relative to the instructional program.

Recommends areas requiring additional evaluation for study by the staff.

Superintendent

Makes recommendations relative to the scope of the instructional program.

Assigns instructors for the various instructional areas.

Develops in-service training programs for the improvement of instruction.

Develops testing programs and other procedures for evaluation of the effectiveness of the instructional program.

Develops procedures for the selection and evaluation of textbooks, audio-visual aids, and other instructional materials.

Gives leadership to the program for the constant evaluation and revision of the program of studies.

Provides leadership for the study of the adequacy of the program of studies and the needs for additions or amendments to it, freely using expert consultants.

FINANCIAL FUNCTIONS

Board of Education

Approves and adopts an annual budget which determines necessary tax levies.

Proposes bond issues to the public for vote.

Adopts regulations for purchasing supplies and equipment.

Adopts standards and passes upon the procedures of financial accounting.

Approves all purchases over $2,000.

Reviews an annual audit of the school district accounts and business procedures.

Superintendent

Presents and interprets to the Board an annual budget proposal.

Analyzes and interprets to the Board long range financial needs and proposals.

Administers the budget and keeps, insofar as possible, all expenditures within its limits.

Directs the system of financial accounting and the activities of those involved in the business department.

Supervises the program for the purchasing of supplies and equipment.

Makes regular periodic reports to the Board relative to financial conditions of the school district.

SCHOOL PLANT FUNCTIONS

Board of Education

Decides what construction should be undertaken.

Decides upon major building renovations, maintenance policies, and additions after considering recommendations from the superintendent.

Purchases school sites.

Employs school architects, as needed.

Employs consultants to advise it on plant needs.

Superintendent

Analyzes and recommends to the Board on school plant needs using consultants as needed.

Develops educational specifications for school buildings.

Works with the architect in the planning of school buildings.

Recommends regarding maintenance needs.

PUPIL PERSONNEL FUNCTIONS

Board of Education

Determines general policies affecting students.

Authorizes the establishment of special classes or schools for atypical children or children with special needs.

Determines general requirements for graduation in accordance with the law.

Provides for the protection of health through school lunch programs, medical examinations, employment of nurses and medical advisers.

Makes regulations regarding corporal punishment, truancy, vandalism, attendance, etc.

Superintendent

Administers the activities of all instructional and guidance personnel.

Directs the policies for pupil discipline.

Directs the classification, promotion, and graduation of pupils.

Directs research programs to determine achievements and needs of pupils.

Develops a program for providing needs for atypical children.

Develops and directs an adequate pupil record system.

Reports to the Board relative to the effectiveness of pupil personnel policies.

PUBLIC RELATIONS FUNCTIONS

Board of Education

Represents community attitudes and values in educational planning and policy development.

Supports the school administration before critical groups in the community and reserves evaluation of the superintendent for executive sessions.

Superintendent

Directs a program for keeping the citizens of the community adequately informed of school developments and problems.

Interprets the program and activities of the schools before various community groups.

Works with parent groups and other organizations interested

Board of Education	**Superintendent**
Represents the schools in various community functions.	in and concerned for the welfare of the schools.
	Makes an annual report on the school program and policies for the Board of Education and the community.
	Meets with representatives of the press to provide information needed for keeping the people of the community informed.

EVALUATION

Board of Education	**Superintendent**
Evaluates periodically, with the superintendent, the work of the superintendent. This should be done in executive session with reports made to the public as deemed desirable.	Evaluates the work of all personnel for the Board in executive session. He also evaluates the instructional program, finances and budgeting and all other aspects of the school program.
Evaluates all other programs of the school system based upon the superintendent's reports and reports of other staff members.	

A natural area of difficulty in maintaining smooth superintendent-Board relationships is in dealing with problems that arise within a school system. Citizens of the community often will mention problems to members of the Board of Education. The board member then faces the question of how he should deal with this problem. If he takes action to solve the problem, he infringes upon the administrative function of the superintendent. If, instead, he calls the problem to the attention of the superintendent, he has fulfilled his initial responsibility. The superintendent then has the responsibility of dealing with the problem and reporting the consequences of his actions. Individual board members can promise no particular solution to a problem, but can only promise that the problem will be investigated and handled by the administration. The administration assumes the responsibility for reporting how the problem was handled. This report may be made to the entire Board on certain occasions, but may be only to the individual board member raising the question in certain other cases. This is often a case of judgment by the superintendent and can sometimes lead to misunderstandings no matter which way the judgment is made. If an aggrieved person is not satisfied with the solution to the problem he should ask for time on the agenda of the next meeting to present the matter to the Board for further consideration.

The superintendent, on the other hand, has a responsibility to inform the Board whenever an administrative decision or problem appears to be of such significance that the Board might ultimately become involved in the situation. It is generally difficult to predict these situations accurately, but the superintendent should make every effort to do so in these particular cases.

The Board of Education should have contacts regarding school matters with the professional staff only through the superintendent of schools. The superintendent should be in a position to make all necessary contacts directly with the professional staff. As the executive officer of the Board of Education, he is the point of contact between the professional staff and the Board. All problems connected with the members of the professional staff should be handled by the superintendent and reported to the Board.

The Board of Education, as the agency designated by the state and the local citizenry, is charged with the responsibility for serving the interests of the people of the local school district and the state. The Board is charged also with the responsibility for the welfare of the teachers and other staff members whose lives are dedicated to the education of children and youth. The superintendent of schools shares these charges and these dedications.

The Board of Education has a unique responsibility in determining the broad general policies under which the school system will function. The Board's principal function, other than adopting operational policies, is the selection of the superintendent of schools.

The superintendent of schools has a unique role in that he is the executive officer of the Board of Education and is also the leader of the professional staff; hence he is responsible to the Board of Education. His primary responsibility, however, is to the boys and girls of the school system. All other responsibilities fall in line after his responsibility to children and young people. The roles of the Board of Education and the superintendent must not only be clearly understood, but definitely practiced to insure the best possible school program. The important factor lies in the mutual acceptance of roles — the basic relationship of the Board as a unit with the superintendent as their chief administrative officer.

If the school system is to prepare future generations to find answers to the problems that perplex our society, the leadership of the school system must continue to be strengthened. This will be done when the Board and the superintendent, in a spirit of mutual understanding and confidence, form a strong and enduring partnership based upon a clear understanding of their respective roles and are dedicated to the betterment of the local school system.

Review of Suggested Procedures

1. Define the powers and duties of the Board as accurately as possible.
2. Determine the commitment of the community to education.
3. Establish a procedure for strengthening that commitment.
4. Develop an understanding of the role of the Board and the role of the superintendent in the school system.
5. Establish an understanding of procedures to be followed in dealing with problems arising in the school system.

11

Initiating and Selling New Programs: The Middle School as an Example

School superintendents are often faced with the need for selling new programs. These programs may be in curriculum or instruction, finance, school building construction, or other allied areas. It is fairly well accepted today that the superintendent of schools is a chief change agent for a school system. He is in the best possible position to institute needed change within the school system. This is possible because of the uniqueness of the position he holds. As a superintendent, he wears many hats. He holds the responsibility for leadership of the professional staff. He is the executive officer of the Board of Education. He represents the school system to the people of the community. He is a financier, operating one of the largest businesses in the community. He directs one of the most comprehensive food service operations, operates one of the most varied transportation systems, employs many people of varied skills and abilities, is charged with the construction of new buildings and the maintenance of older ones, requires children to attend school, and holds the responsibility in his hands for the education of all citizens in the community.

The very uniqueness of this position presents a dilemma to the practicing superintendent. He is in the best position to initiate change and to bring about progress, but the complexities and pressures of the job make it difficult for him to accomplish all the things that seem needed and desirable. This dilemma often leads to frustration and confusion for the superintendent as he faces the realities of today's problems on one hand, while he plans for change and future growth and development on the other. He is generally limited by the financial capabilities of the school district while he is challenged by the apparent needs and desires of the community, and his own knowledge of those things which must be improved.

The superintendent today who is going to initiate new programs to his staff, school system, and community must be well organized and have at his disposal the necessary techniques for implementing change. The Board of Education must be considered as an integral part of his planning for such change. The Board must be aware of the need for change, must be kept informed of the study that is underway, and must agree with the procedures to be followed if it is to be expected to adopt the new program offered by the superintendent. The superintendent must not be too far ahead of his board members if he expects their support and encouragement along the way. It is understood that situations vary greatly from one school system to another. The point has been made repeatedly in this book that no two school systems are alike. There are, however, enough similarities that a set of general procedures can be suggested for initiating and selling new programs and services within the school system.

This chapter deals with implementing the middle school concept into a school system. This situation is used as an example for three reasons: (1) the middle school concept is an emerging pattern of organization in the country which many superintendents are now facing; (2) it is a major organizational and curricular change; (3) the procedures followed might be applicable to other desired changes. It is recognized that it is not possible to itemize all the steps necessary for implementing change, so the major focus of this chapter will be on general long range planning and on the involvement of the Board of Education in the program.

For purposes of illustration the necessary steps for initiating this new program are divided into three stages. There is rarely a clear-cut dividing line between the stages of pre-planning, preparation, and implementation, but it can be helpful in long range planning to make the distinction well known.

STAGE I

PRELIMINARY PLANNING

The Planning Team and the Superintendent's Cabinet

The superintendent meets regularly with members of his planning team. If the school system is of sufficient size, he will have a regular pattern for meeting with various departments or branches of the school system. The Superintendent would first discuss the possibility of the middle school concept for his school system with the members of his planning team or superintendent's cabinet, or central office staff, or whatever group the superintendent counts on as his immediate advisory and planning group. In this series of meetings with the planning team, the superintendent should initiate discussions concerning the problem of building utilization in the school system, and the question of curriculum development. After several preliminary discussions concerning the possibility of the middle school concept as a means of providing better building utilization and a new approach to curriculum, the superintendent can determine from the discussions when the stage is set to begin serious study of the problem. Since the program involving the middle school concept is going to revolve around curricular change and building utilization, it is now time to implement a study of both of these areas. At this point the superintendent can outline for his staff member who heads the division of instruction, the need for a study of the curricular offerings and organization, methodology, and content, currently being utilized in the junior high schools. This study should concentrate on the current status of curriculum organization and how it might be improved by a different approach that might accompany the middle school program. The staff member in charge of administration, or in charge of business affairs, might be assigned the responsibility of conducting a study of building utilization. This would probably include site maps for each individual school, a diagram of each school building accompanied by dimensions, square footage, and other necessary information. The building utilization report should portray the number of periods per day each room in the building is being used and the number of students assigned to the rooms.

Once the study is outlined by the superintendent and the planning team, the staff members responsible for segments of the study may then assign their responsibilities and apportion the work as they deem advisable. It is important that deadlines be set for these materials, otherwise it does not seem enough importance is attached to the study and the study tends to drag on without any decisiveness or sense of direction. The established deadline should be reasonable and not impose a real hardship on staff members who already have full schedules of duties. It is appropriate at this point to issue a word of warning concerning studies that are made by staff members and the establishment of deadlines. It can be extremely frustrating to a staff member who is already loaded down with a great number of responsibilities which demand completion by a certain date. It is likewise frustrating if an individual staff member completes an assignment and does it well and on time, and no mention is ever made of the contribution he has presented. It is important to recognize the staff members who contribute to an important study.

Keep the Board Informed

As the superintendent completes his preliminary discussion with the planning team and assigns the responsibilities for study, it is important to present this information to the Board of Education. This presentation could well be a part of a weekly memorandum or it could be done at a regular meeting of the Board. It would seem more desirable at this point, however, for the superintendent to inform the Board by memorandum. At this point he is seldom ready for publicity on the matter through the newspapers, and other media. In the memorandum to the Board, the superintendent should be certain that he reports to the Board the need for this study, the procedures that will be followed in the study, and what will be done with the information and material once it is compiled. The superintendent would do well at this point to list the expected date or month at which he would outline the study in detail to the Board. This would occur at some subsequent meeting and this preliminary memorandum would serve as an introduction to the study and would also serve as a means of informing the Board concerning a very important action of the staff. While it is important to keep the Board informed on all stages of initiating new programs, it is particularly important in the early stages of planning that the Board see the need for study and know specifically how the study is being approached.

Long Range Plans for Implementing the Study

The superintendent and his planning team need to decide together on the procedures that will be followed throughout the study and at what point in the study other personnel will become involved. It is important at this point to establish the time and procedures for involvement of the central office staff in various aspects of the study. Decision should be made concerning when the involvement of principals will occur. How will the review of current literature be accomplished and how will this be disseminated to staff members? Visits to middle schools now in operation should be considered at this point. Particular emphasis should be given to the study of general curriculum design in the middle schools. The planning team and the staff should tentatively identify some outside consultants who might be of specific help in the planning and study of the middle school concept. It is necessary that the superintendent stress to the staff the importance of the study since it will involve a major organizational and curricular change for the school system.

Staff Report to the Board

As soon as the study is completed, the superintendent should arrange for time to present the study to the Board of Education in a regular meeting. It would appear to be in order for the superintendent to introduce the study to the Board and to have specific sections of the study presented by those staff members who had responsibility in those areas. This study should be presented in either notebook or binder form so the Board could use it as a continuing reference as the middle school study progresses. The report on building utilization would have implications for housing students in the future, and the general report on curriculum would present a survey of both the strengths and the weaknesses of the current curricular approach.

Following the presentation by the staff to the Board concerning the study, it is important for the Board of Education, at this point, to take definitive action concerning whether or not the superintendent should proceed with plans for organizing the school system in accordance with the study that was made. In essence, the Board would authorize the administration to conduct an independent study of the middle school concept, the advantages for school organization in changing from a 6-3-3 to a 5-3-4 plan, and the necessary changes in philosophy and curriculum. This action by the Board should set the stage for decisive steps by the administration in the future.

Community Awareness and Involvement

It is appropriate at this point for the community to be made aware of the study that is underway by the school administration. The Board will generally recognize the importance of involving the community in such a major step. In many school situations, it would be advisable at this point to select a community advisory committee to work with the staff and to perform the specific function of reacting to ideas uncovered in the study by the staff and to present the lay citizen's point of view concerning the possibility of the school system's adopting the middle school concept. The Board and the administration should follow the generally accepted rules for the use of advisory committees. In this case the committee should be appointed for this specific reason with the understanding that the committee would be expected to serve for a specified period of time and that following completion of its task, the committee would be disbanded. It should be emphasized that the committee should be appointed by the Board of Education with the advice of the superintendent, and should be appointed to work through the superintendent and not directly with the Board. This advisory committee can play a very important role in the development of the study of the middle school concept. It is very important that the superintendent and his staff understand the community reaction that might be developing as the school system conducts this particular study.

As the school administration and staff members make progress in the study, the chairman of the advisory committee and the superintendent will together present their findings and opinions to the Board. The superintendent and Board will recognize the importance of involving the community and keeping the community well informed, but will also recognize that there are dangers in advisory committees if they are not properly constituted and organized. An advisory committee will be of little real value if members feel they are selected merely to support everything the administration develops. The committee can, however, play an important role if it understands its mission and can operate in a positive manner which will aid the Board and the administration in understanding community reaction and in assisting in informing the public about the program. The school system's procedures for informing the public on all school matters should be utilized efficiently so that the public will be kept informed on the development of the study.

STAGE II
PREPARATION

Concentrated Study

In studying the middle school concept it can be very helpful if someone is assigned the responsibility of compiling a review of the literature on the middle school. A number of books and periodicals are available concerning the middle school development and it would be most helpful to staff members to have this material condensed into a readable form. This, along with other studies, can be very helpful as the system adopts its overall philosophy concerning the middle school program. This review of literature, or study guide, should be made available to those staff members involved in the study, to members of the Board of Education, members of the citizens' advisory committee, and to those members of the press who normally cover school activities. This study guide would, of course, be reviewed by the superintendent prior to its release, and dissemination of the study guide to specific individuals should be determined by the superintendent and the planning team.

It is important during this period of concentrated study that the calendar for long range implementation of the program be established. This calendar should be developed by the planning team and the staff, and should consider the various time factors involved in making the study. The calendar should be presented to the Board and discussed by the Board so that everyone is aware of the schedule being pursued. It should be made clear that this is a tentative schedule which will be subject to the demands of the school system and various emergency situations that arise, but it should be the intention of the Board and the administration together to implement the calendar as nearly as possible. The calendar should not be a straight jacket but it should serve as a guide and a help in completing the study.

Part of the concentrated study should include visitations to operational middle schools. The selection of schools to be visited should be made very carefully, so that unique features, current curricular programs, building design, staffing patterns, schedule of students from class, and building construction can be studied. Whenever possible the board members should be involved in some of the visitations. This enables members of the Board to get a first-hand picture not only of what the middle school should be, but of some of the problems involved in implementing a major organizational and curricular change.

Training of Administrators

Principals, supervisor, and coordinators will play a very important part in the operation of the middle school program. Special training must be designed for these key staff members if everyone is to develop a common philosophy and outlook on the development of the program. It is suggested that a series of workshops be organized dealing with the philosophy of the middle school program, the changes it represents, and procedures to be followed in developing and implementing the program. These workshops should utilize the services of specified consultants who have experience in the middle school program. These consultants might be found at various universities and at operational middle schools.

The workshops should be the kind that involve the participants actively in all of the activities so that the workshops are practical and useful to all concerned.

A key decision at this point concerns the selection of participants for the workshops. It would seem important to involve all junior high school principals. It is important also to consider and decide whether elementary and senior high school principals should also be involved, and if so, the extent to which they should be involved. The selection of principals for specific middle schools will be a very key decision. If the selection of these administrators is obvious, and if personnel are available to fill these positions, this decision can be made. If there is some doubt as to the appointment of principals for the schools, a statement should be made as to when such a decision will be announced. The calendar adopted by the Board should indicate when this decision will be made. It is important that the principals for the middle schools be selected prior to the selection of the staff.

Selection of Staff

The selection of staff members for the newly organized middle schools is an extremely important step. These are the personnel who will make the middle school program succeed and who will carry the major load in planning and implementing the specifics of the program. It is important that time be allotted for a concentrated workshop involving the principal and his staff members. At this workshop the staff should have sufficient time to prepare its own statement of philosophy and develop its goals and objectives for the program. These workshops might be scheduled at various regular periods of time during the spring with a concentrated workshop in the summer prior to the opening of school in the fall. The problems of specific school schedules, assignment of students, grouping patterns, activity programs, athletics, special events, and many others, must be decided by the staff and the principal as they plan for the coming year. It is imperative that the staff feel as well prepared as possible for the beginning of the middle school program with the opening of school in September.

Board Decisions

During this preparation period the Board will make a number of important decisions. The Board will pass on the selection of principals and staff members. It will approve the workshops as planned. It will have an understanding of the programs that are designed for public information. Board members may all participate in programs for Parent Teacher Associations, parent groups of the students involved, and civic clubs. The Board during this period of time will also adopt officially the middle school program of organization and establish a definite date for implementation. The Board will probably need to hold a series of public meetings on this middle school program so as to afford opportunity for citizens to be heard and to have their questions answered.

Student and Community Involvement

It is very important during this period of preparation that the students who will be affected by this program be given special consideration concerning their suggestions, ideas, attitudes and feelings. It would be particularly helpful if those selected as principals for the middle schools could meet with various student groups to aid in their understanding of the program. While the matter will not be discussed in any detail in this book, the school administration will want to give this matter very serious consideration and be certain that the students are aware of the philosophy of the school system concerning the middle school program and the specific ways that this concept will produce a better educational opportunity for the students involved.

At the same time the community must be informed and a conscientious effort made to determine the feelings of the community and to sense the reaction of the community to the total program. Brochures, written explanations, public meetings, illustrations can all be helpful in informing the public. It is particularly important that the parents of those students who will be in the middle schools understand the basic concepts of the middle school program.

STAGE III
IMPLEMENTATION

Pre-School Concentrated Workshop

In planning for the implementation of a middle school program, as with any other major organizational change, it is important that the specific staff for the middle school have as much time together as possible. The myriad details of starting a school year are compounded when a new organization goes into effect. Those school systems that normally operate a pre-school session for all staff members would do well to designate the majority of that time for staff members to be in their individual schools working with their principals and curriculum specialists as they prepare for this new organization. The staff will need time to re-orient their team members, curriculum committee assignments, and overall coordination that may have been lost over the summer vacation. Central office staff members should make a special effort to be of assistance to those schools where the new program and new organization is to be implemented.

Student and Parent Orientation

With the start of school a new philosophy and organizational pattern, and a different approach to curriculum, are going to be implemented. It is vital to the success of the program that the students of the school have a basic understanding of the purpose of the new organization and how this particular approach will be of benefit to them. Each school principal and staff will need to work out the best way to accomplish this, but it is appropriate for the administration to remind principals of the necessity of this student orientation.

Early in the school year it is most desirable to have an explanatory program for all parents that explains the details of the operation of this new program. The Parent Teacher Association can be very helpful in organizing such a session for parents so that there is a common understanding on the part of the parents as to the purpose of the new approach, what the parents must expect, and how they can be of assistance to their children in this new organization.

Operation of the Program

The superintendent must keep the Board informed of all of the significant details of the operational aspect of the middle school program. The Board should have a basic understanding of such important things as grouping procedures, scheduling, team teaching and planning, guidance and counseling, special school activities, and reporting to parents. It is very helpful if the superintendent can arrange for the Board to visit in one or more of the middle schools as they become operational. County-wide staff members, in adapting the philosophy of providing help and assistance to the middle school, should be available to staff members as they are needed. The county-wide personnel must recognize that the new organization will present special problems that will require special attention.

Evaluation

Evaluation of a new program should be accomplished over a period of time. The superintendent might well assign a team of personnel from the county-wide staff to assist in the periodic evaluation of the program. It should be stressed that this evaluation is not for the purpose of threatening the status or position of teachers and administrators, but is for the purpose of providing program improvement and for assisting staff members with specific problems that arise. It is conceivable that this evaluation team might visit the middle school three or four times as a team during the school year in order to assist the staff members in the implementation of this new program. The superintendent would want to establish with the Board a regular report on the status of the new program and its efficiency in meeting the problems of the students and the staff, and in improving the general learning situation. In this evaluation the superintendent would want also to report to the Board on the impact this new program would have on both the elementary and senior high programs. The evaluation should be recognized as an integral part of the total planning process. If done properly, and with the right philosophy, evaluation can be viewed by the staff members as a real help in the program. If done improperly, it can pose a serious threat to the total school program.

SUMMARY

Initiating and selling a program, such as the middle school concept described in this chapter, is a complex operation. It cannot succeed without careful planning, good organization, an informed and understanding Board, and good operational techniques. The calendar enclosed at the end of the chapter for planning, study, and implementing the middle school concept may be of some assistance in reviewing the approach described in this chapter. It should be emphasized again that this is not intended as a guideline for all school systems but merely as a suggested means of accomplishing a major change in a school system.

Review of Suggested Procedures

1. Recognize the unique position of leadership held by the superintendent.
2. Planning and initiating new programs demands involvement of staff, students, Board and community.
3. Preliminary planning should outline the total approach to the new program.
4. Establish a calendar for implementation of the program.
5. Provide for systematic evaluation.
6. Remember that the Board is charged with the final decision and responsibility. Keep them informed of all developments.

CALENDAR FOR PLANNING, STUDYING AND IMPLEMENTING THE MIDDLE SCHOOL CONCEPT

January, 19___

1. As part of continuous problem of housing students and maintaining adequate and relevant curriculum, discuss with Planning Team and Superintendent's Cabinet the problems of building utilization and curriculum development.

2. Inform Board in weekly memo of the need for the study and reasons for the study.

February, 19___

Assign specific responsibilities for building utilization study (Business or Administrative Division) and curriculum (Division of Instruction).

March, 19___

1. Report to Board on current status of building utilization, housing of students in the future, and general curriculum survey of strengths and weaknesses.

2. Get Board authorization to conduct study of middle school concept, its advantages for school organization in changing from 6-3-3 to 5-3-4 plan, and the necessary changes in philosophy and curriculum.

April, 19___

Joint Board and Staff visitation to operational middle school. Observe program, organization, staffing pattern, scheduling of students and classes, construction, etc.

May, 19___

1. Recommend for Board adoption a calendar and plan for studying, adopting, and implementing the middle school concept. Study can be stopped at any time administration or Board determines program is not feasible.

2. Superintendent outlines his organization for accomplishing the study.

July, 19___

Progress report to Board by staff members assigned specific responsibilities in the study.

September, 19___

1. Study Guide on Middle School Concept prepared by Superintendent and staff, distributed to Board and staff members involved. This would include the philosophy of the middle school, a review of current literature, and specific areas of concern such as teaching methodology, curriculum, needs of students of middle school age, and scheduling.

2. Recommendation for Board appointment of a Citizens Study Committee on the middle school to study the program and offer reactions as parents and members of the community, and to offer further suggestions for studying and implementing the program.

October, November, and December, 19___

Work with school staffs and Citizens Study Committee.

Following year: January, 19___

Report of Citizens Study Committee to Superintendent and then to Board.

February, 19___

Board adoption of middle school plan. Establishment of calendar for implementation of program in September, 19___.

February — May, 19___

Workshops for all principals, all subject area supervisors, on middle school concept, programs for PTA's, parent groups of students involved, civic clubs. General program to inform public concerning middle school program. Work with students to give them understanding of the new program.

March, 19___

Select administrators with specific responsibility for middle school program. Identify schools to be designated as middle schools and appoint principals.

April, 19___

Select staff for middle schools. Establish special budget for middle schools. Order special equipment, materials, and furniture needed for individualized instruction, team-teaching, etc.

June 19___   Ten-day workshop for staff of each middle
                           school with consultants as needed. Orienta-
                           tion, grouping of students, final curriculum
                           decisions, best use of facilities, establish class
                           modular schedules, etc.

July, 19___   Report to Board on results of workshop and
                           plans for pre-school planning.

August, 19___   1. Pre-school workshop for all staff includes
                           special planning time for middle schools and
                           supervisory staff.

                           2. Board visitation to middle schools to view
                           facilities, grouping, curriculum plans, etc.

September, 19___   Begin operation of middle school program.

Following year: Mid-year progress report to Board with em-
January, 19___   phasis on relationship of middle school to
                           both elementary and senior high.

July, 19___   End of year evaluation to Board.

12

Increasing
the Effectiveness
of the Board

The effectiveness of the Board of Education in a local community can be improved by following certain patterns of action. It is important to note that this improvement can occur only when the members of the Board and the superintendent are convinced of the need for improvement. There must exist within the Board an attitude which is desirous of improvement in the effectiveness and the productivity of the Board. The Board and the superintendent must have an understanding that they are going to analyze the meetings and the activities of the Board and produce changes as they are needed and as they are desirable, in order to accomplish more effective board meetings. While several items have been discussed in previous chapters that might be helpful in this regard, a few strategic points are covered in this chapter concerning increased efficiency of the Board.

Analyze Your Own Meetings

Once the Board and the superintendent have adopted an attitude which is desirous of improvement and change, the next step is to analyze the activities of the Board as reflected in its public meetings. This analysis should determine how effective the board meetings are in terms of accomplishing the business of the school system. In this analysis the Board should pay particular attention to the planning that precedes the meeting, the actual conduct of the meeting, and the interpretation of that meeting to the citizens and to the staff.

In analyzing the effectiveness of your school board meetings, the first step is to determine the quality of the planning that precedes the meeting. Does the superintendent involve key members of his staff in the planning, and is the planning done with an eye toward the long range needs of the school system as well as satisfying the immediate demands? The superintendent and the Board, in analyzing this planning, will want to determine if the board members have sufficient opportunity to participate in the planning and to place items on the agenda when they deem it necessary.

It is extremely important that the Board and the superintendent assess the quality of communications between the superintendent and the Board. It is worthwhile for the superintendent and the Board to meet together on occasion to discuss communications and the role that each plays in planning and conducting school board meetings.

The superintendent and members of the Board want to be certain that the agenda is well planned and that it follows a consistent format. The superintendent should know whether his board members feel that he is providing them adequate background information on all subjects coming before the Board for action. If the meetings are lengthy, can anything be done to shorten them without decreasing the efficiency of the Board? Could a time schedule be helpful or should the Board meet more often? Or can the Board streamline some of its activities?

The Board and superintendent will need to analyze the physical setting for the meeting to be sure that the facilities are adequate to accommodate a crowd when necessary, and that the acoustics and other physical arrangements are the best that can be made under the circumstances available. A competent secretary to record the activities of the Board is essential, along with the use of recording equipment for assistance to the secretary and to the superintendent and board members.

The superintendent will want to be certain that he is exercising his responsibility for educational leadership in meetings of the Board. In looking for ways to increase the effectiveness of board meetings, both the board members and the superintendent will want to make sure that major issues facing the school system, and consequently facing the Board, are attacked by some definite recommendation for action by the superintendent.

The Board may be having effective meetings, while at the same time ineffective press relations may give the Board a bad public image. If this should be the case, the Board would need to analyze its relations with representatives of the media. The superintendent needs to make certain that he has a good understanding with the media as to the role that each plays and the procedures they will follow in the entire area of news releases and publicity.

It is essential that evaluation be a regular part of the procedures of the Board and the superintendent working together. Evaluation of the meetings is an important step toward improvements. It is particularly important that individual board members analyze their own contributions to the meeting. Are you as well informed as you should be? Do you understand the issues? Do you know the consequences of alternative courses of action? Do you know the feelings of your constituents in the community? All of these questions are necessary and they demand answers by both the board members and the superintendent. Such a self-analysis is the first step toward increased efficiency in meetings of the Board of Education.

Learn from Others

The local Board of Education and the superintendent can accomplish a great deal through communication with other Boards and other superintendents. They can exchange ideas and practices, and discuss problems which are common to them all. Superintendents do this quite regularly by the very nature of the positions they hold. They are thrown together quite often in the solving of problems of mutual concern and often consult each other on matters of importance. A great deal can be accomplished by board members through attendance at meetings of their state associations and the National School Board's Association, and by superintendents through attendance at the State Superintendent's Association and the American Association of School Administrators. These organizations are committed to assisting board members and superintendents with the problems that confront them. It is a real advantage to local board members and superintendents to exchange ideas and practices with other board members and administrators.

Preparation Programs for Superintendents

Colleges and universities today are assessing their preparation programs for school superintendents. Many of the universities are accepting the fact that the superintendency today is a different position than it was a few short years ago. Few superintendents have had any training in dealing with some of today's modern problems, such as negotiations, student activism, strikes and walk-outs, pressure tactics, and community dynamics. More and more universities are facing up to the necessity of revising their preparation programs. This is a good step in the right direction. In addition to the preparation programs, however, universities must be aware of the need for in-service education programs for superintendents. Those superintendents who have been out of college for a number of years are gaining experience in dealing with current problems on a day to day basis. The universities should definitely take advantage of the experience of these superintendents in the preparation of future superintendents. Both pre-service and in-service education of school superintendents should involve some concentration on the role superintendents play in effective and productive school board meetings. For some reason or other this item has been missing from most preparation programs for school superintendents. Those preparation programs should include practice in planning and conducting meetings of a Board of Education. Simulation can be very helpful in this area. Many new superintendents are simply not prepared to conduct effective board meetings because the matter was never given any attention in their preparation programs.

A number of universities are working cooperatively today with state school Boards' associations and state administrators' associations to provide in-service programs for both board members and superintendents. These can be very effective programs if they are relevant to the needs of the board members and the superintendent. These programs should be planned cooperatively with a definite involvement of practicing board members and superintendents so that the in-service training sessions are useful and helpful to the board members.

A Final Word

Public education is a vital function of our society. At no time in our history has education been so important as it is today. It is important to the individual as he prepares to cope with the world in which he will live, as he prepares to earn a living, and as he prepares to change and improve his environment. Education is important to society because it is our best hope for a better world. The Board of Education plays a key role in the development of education in the local community. In this regard the size and complexity of the school system has no relevancy. The key role is established regardless of the size or location of the school system. Continued attention to the needs of the students is the first priority of the Board and will, in itself, constitute a major step toward more productive board meetings. No citizen participates in a more worthwhile activity than that of service on a Board of Education. The effectiveness of a superintendent or a board member will influence the lives of many individuals.

Index